for All
the Wrong
Reasons

SHEZKY
you are so nice!
THANK God you are
in my LIFe
ABRAZO's TO you

For All the Wrong Reasons by Dan Benavidez

Published by Del Hayes Press, 1690 Estates Parkway, Allen, TX 75002.
972-727-3693. First edition. Visit our website at www.delhayespress.com
for information on bulk orders.

ISBN-10 0-9822706-6-6
ISBN-13 978-0-9822706-6-0

Front cover photograph used with permission of the Times-Call newspaper
of Longmont, Colorado.

Back cover photograph of author used with permission of Debe
Richardson, Longmont, Colorado.

Printed in the United States of America

Cover and book design
by Clint Hayes

For my familia: Mama B, my angel who believed in me, and Celia, Elaine, Aja, and Layla for your patience and strength through it all.

Acknowledgements

I am grateful to my other "family" for their unwavering support: Linda (Lyndy) Leary, mi querida amiga, mi gringa hermana—without your word magic, editing, and the occasional kick in the pants, the book would never have been finished; Elza Lynne Kruger, my South African friend and special mentor, for helping me sort it all out and maintain some degree of sanity throughout the process; David Brenner, a lifetime friend whose honest advice and beautiful foreword to this book mean more to me than I can say; Tim Sturm, who is not only a true friend but a brother of my heart; Lois Linser, my Golden Ponds buddy whose reviews and guidance were so meaningful; Mike Butler, a true leader and a spot-on model of a person doing things for all the right reasons; Julia and Scott Pirnack, for helping me keep my focus and do the right thing for the right reasons when writing about racial discrimination; Jeannette Holtham, because you're special, you taught me, and helped ever so much. And lastly, but certainly not least, to all those other "earth angels" along the way who provided opportunities and opened doors for this Mexican boy from the 'hood: Gracias. Thank you all from my heart.

Foreword

What in the world would a Jewish comedian raised in Philadelphia have in common with a Mexican raised in the barrios of the Southwest? Well, as a starter, how about over fifty years of unwavering friendship, the kind that two blood brothers experience? Daniel Celio Benavidez, or "Benny" as I have known him, and I are brothers—hermanos.

I met Benny when we were stationed in the army in Panzer Kaserne billets in the small town of Boeblingen, Germany, a short distance from Stuttgart. He was a super friendly, super lively, super fun guy who gathered friends like a magnet gathers metal shavings. I was lucky to be one of them.

He and I immediately hit it off and became best buddies, along with a pretty wild, eclectic collection of other soldiers from all corners of the states, all walks of civilian life and all ethnic and racial backgrounds, including Mexicans, Blacks, Jews, Irish, Italians, Greeks, WASPs and even an Arab.

Benny and I and an Italian, also from Philly, Al Benedetto, were an inseparable clique within the gang. We went on leaves in Europe having the best times, very few of which would be proper to put into print. We also hung out wherever we were stationed and it is these times about which I'll write, mainly because this is when I met the true man we often called "Blood and Guts."

This was back when Germany was a decade-plus over World War II. But not over hating Jews. They still hunted young American Jewish soldiers, but these times without weapons and not in overwhelming numbers. I was a tough kid from a tough neighborhood and full of hate for Nazis for murdering six million Jews, including my European relatives. I asked my father to send me a Mezuzah on a chain. He mistakenly thought I had found religion in the army, which was not true. What I did find was an opportunity to silently announce that I was a Jew, a survivor and just one of all others who did, and to announce that what happened would never happen again. So, when Benny and I and some others went into town on a night pass, hitting clubs and dance halls, I wore my Mezuzah hanging outside my shirt for all to see, especially . . .

One night, a few ex-Nazis in the booth behind us started with their anti-Jewish remarks and jokes about killing Jews. All of a sudden, Benny was out of his seat, up on the table and flying over my head, landing on top of the Nazis. We all followed his lead and got a tiny bit of revenge.

This kind of behavior became very common and Benny was almost always the first to explode and one of the best at fighting. Every once in a while I saw Benny go one on one with some soldiers, never saying what provoked him to do it. I thought that maybe he just liked to fight. I grew up with guys who were like that. One night I found out why he had his fists flying.

We had known each other about six months when Benny had too much tequila to drink, not an uncommon occurrence, and I helped him off the floor and led his rubber legs out of the club. I plopped him down on the club's top steps and held my hand on his forehead while he threw up repeatedly. When he got it all out, I held him so he wouldn't fall head first down the cement steps to the pavement below.

He mumbled something I couldn't understand and kept repeating it. I listened closely. Benny was saying, "David, thanks for always treating me as a white man." He hugged me tightly and kept repeating it. I thought he was being funny and laughed, but he started crying, a gut-wrenching cry, tears rolling down his face, his hug getting tighter. I realized that he was serious and asked him what he was talking about. He was white to me. He spoke between his cries and tears.

"Where I'm from, I'm not white. I'm a low life, Mexican, an animal, a piece of shit!"

I never knew Benny was a Mexican. I didn't know what he was and could not have cared less. We didn't persecute Mexicans in Philly. Firstly, we didn't have any, as far as I knew. Secondly, we had Puerto Ricans to persecute, and, of course, Blacks and my people. We didn't need to add Mexicans.

That night I learned that my dear friend was a Mexican and over the next year or so in the army he opened my eyes and heart to the plight of his people, and over the years since then, he has taught me so much more. As these years have passed, one thing that was not news to me or a surprise was his unrelenting, undying dedication to fight for his "people." I have been, am, and always will be so proud of my Mexican brother.

You have the opportunity to learn about the life and the extraordinary man who lived it within these chapters. Don't miss the opportunity.

David Brenner, Comedian
&
Daniel Celio "Blood & Guts" Benavidez

Hermanos

For All the Wrong Reasons

Prologue

"The longest journey is the journey inward."

Dag Hammarskjold

The sun streamed through the window bathing my mother's withered face in a soft glow. As I sat by her bed holding her hand, I wondered at the strength and wisdom looking back at me from those dark eyes. Though grown, I felt once again like a little boy, and I could hide nothing from her. My heart ached with the thought that soon she would pass from this world and I would no longer hear her voice nor see the flash and dance of her eyes when she was happy.

As if sensing my thoughts, she squeezed my hand and asked, her voice cracking slightly, "Mi hijo, my son, tell me what is in your heart."

"Mama, I hurt inside. My soul is tortured. I have been off chasing rainbows, trying to make something of myself, trying to become accepted. It has not been easy, but I guess I made it. I did make it, didn't I, Mama?"

She gazed steadily into my eyes for several moments before speaking. "Is it because I am dying? Is that why you want to tell me this?"

Tears stung the backs of my eyelids. "Oh God, Mama, don't say that!"

She squeezed my hand with a force that surprised me. "Don't worry, mi hijo, it is all right. I am ready to go home. I have found my peace. Now it is time for you to find yours. Tell me."

"Mama, I am a grown man, yet I am still insecure. I still do not know where I am going; I'm just trying to sort myself out. Daddy once told me, 'Don't be a chili picker like your old man. Make something of yourself.' I am not a chili picker! I have made something of myself and I know he would have been so proud of me, but why am I not proud of me? I did it, yes. I made something of myself, but for all the wrong reasons."

The gates of my heart crashed open and all my pain poured out. My mama, my confessor, the heart of our family, listened, her eyes piercing my soul.

"You know, I am ashamed to say this," I confessed, "and please forgive me since you may not understand, but I was not always happy being Mexican. I wanted to be more like the Anglos. I wanted to be brown on the inside but white on the outside so I would fit into their world." I could see that what I said disturbed her, yet she said nothing and I could not stop the words.

"Mama, I messed myself up. I became a big fish in a little pond. However, I became a big fish for all the wrong reasons. Even when I swam in the pond amongst the other big fish, I felt alone, another dark face in the gringo world. I still felt left out and inferior. I wanted so very much to be part of white society and still be proud that I was Mexican but I could not get the two to fit together. I was probably a 'Tio Taco.' I dreamed of becoming a mover and shaker, a person of power and influence mingling with the elite and the educated, and being accepted. I guess I did become a mover and shaker, huh, Mama? But it was no fun, and the acceptance I had dreamed of for so long was not what I perceived it would be. I made a fool of myself, subjugated myself, just to get in the doors that had been closed to me and to my people. I had 'arrived,' but got there for all the wrong reasons."

I paused, took a breath and continued, "Mama, I still hurt. I feel so empty inside. Mamacita, I love you. I know I have not been a good son."

"Oh mi hijo," Mama said. "You have been a good boy. I am so proud of you; I have all your newspaper clippings and I show them to everyone."

"Mamacita, you are so good to me even though I have spent most of my life satisfying my own ego and not being here for you. I even complained about cutting the lawn for you. Oh Mama, please forgive me."

"Son," she said, "you have always been here for me and just knowing that you are a good boy and that I did right in raising you is good enough for me. I know you are on the right path. I know you will find the peace you seek because you care so much about me and our family, and all my vecinos, my neighbors, are so proud of you for what you have done for us and for the Mexicans, so don't be so hard on yourself."

My tears turned to sobs. "Oh, Mamacita. Te quiero con todo mi corazón. I love you with all my heart. Shame on me. Mea culpa, mea culpa, mea maxima culpa for my weakness!" I suddenly remembered Emiliano Zapata, my Mexican hero: "It is better to die standing on your feet than to be living on your knees." The words rang again in my ears.

"No more on my knees, Mama! No more on my knees! Don't cry for me, mi mamacita. I'll be all right now. I know what color I am on the outside and the inside and I am okay with it. It is time I give up being a mover and shaker, a warrior for power, and start down the path to becoming a warrior for peace, striving for a more peaceful blending, to see what humanity's colors look like. We are all the same color inside. Rest now, mi angel dulce. I love you so very much."

Chapter 1

"If you do not go within, you go without."

Neale Donald Walsch

Had anyone tried to tell me, on that cool autumn afternoon in my mother's kitchen, that her days were numbered, I would not have believed them. She was so vital and, well, she was mi mamacita, my mama, the one I could always count on. And I was her hijo, her son.

In the months to follow I would have to face many deeply buried memories, some of which I hoped never to face again in this lifetime. My caring for her during those final sad and painful months became a poignant journey of remembering, an emotional catharsis and eventual healing for this Latino man.

It all began so innocently when my sister, Lee, made a casual comment to me. "You know, Dan, Mom complained to me that she was having trouble kneeling when we went to mass this morning. She said she has a lump on her knee."

Unconcerned I replied, "Oh, Lee, I'm sure it's nothing; she probably just bumped it on something."

Lee was unconvinced. "I am not so sure, Dan. It worries me. You know how mom is: She *never* complains about anything, so for her to make a comment like this . . . Maybe I should take her to the doctor. What do you think?"

I could hear the concern in my sister's voice and decided to go along with her even though I thought there was no real reason for it. "Okay, sis, if you think so. It probably isn't anything serious, but if it will make you feel better I'll drop by Mom's place and take a look at her, okay?"

I walked into my mother's house on Bowen Street to the rich aroma of her special red chili with all its delicious spices. It never failed to bring back memories of my childhood that was poor in material things but rich in love and good cooking. I crept up behind her.

"Hey, Mamacita. Que pasa?" (How goes it?)

My mother turned, startled, then smiled. "Ah, mi hijo, it is good to see you and why do you wait so long to visit me?" She shook her finger at me while faking a frown. I grabbed her in a hug. "Ah, Mama, you know I always come by when I need a good beans and chili fix." Releasing her I held up three fingers. "How many fingers do you see?"

"Well, *two*, of course, hijo." She grinned, tilting her head. I made a great show of being surprised. "Wow! Mom, you got it right again; you never fail to amaze me." We both laughed. It was a silly finger game that we had been playing with each other for years and she loved it. For some reason I loved it too, maybe because it was just between us.

Attempting to sound casual I remarked, "Let me see your knee, mom. Lee tells me you have a bump on it."

"Oh, hijo, it isn't anything, really. I must have bumped myself on the stove." She shrugged and turned back to her pot of chili. I remembered my promise to Lee and persisted. "I know, but let me take a look anyway, okay?" She modestly raised her dress slightly up on her thigh and I examined the small bump on her knee that looked like a very big pimple. I gently pressed it between my thumb and forefinger. It was soft and pliable to my pressure and I watched my mom's face for any obvious reaction to pain. "Does that hurt, mi mamacita?"

"No, no, hijo. It's just a little sore but it doesn't hurt much." Feeling satisfied I reassured my mother. "Okay, I really don't think it amounts to anything and I wouldn't worry about it if I were you. But you know Lee is concerned and would like you to see a doctor, so why don't you go with her just to be on the safe side?" I started to tease her then. "Hey, Mama, I think I know what really happened to your knee." She gave me one of her exasperated "What now?" looks. "Oh really, hijo? Tell me, what *did* happen to my knee?"

"Well, Mom, some of your amigas (girlfriends) told me that you were out at the cantina last night throwing silver coins around like there was no tomorrow, buying everyone cervezas (beers) and tequilas and singing las mañanitas at the top of your lungs. You were dancing on top of a table with a lamp shade on your head when you fell off the table and bumped your knee on a damn bar stool. What a wicked girl you are, Mamacita."

I saw that Mom almost laughed but instead she shook her head and gave me a stern look. "Danny, mi querido hijo (my darling son), por favor, please, don't use that kind of bad language."

I feigned a surprised look. "What bad words? Oh, do you mean 'damn'? That's not a bad word."

She looked up from the soup ladle she was holding in her hands and waved it at me. "In my house, mi hijo, it is so. Por favor, don't use that word."

I threw up my hands in a phony surrender. "Okay, Mamacita, I give up. No more 'damns' in your house, okay?"

She gave me "the look" and turned back to the chili she was stirring, muttering under her breath. "Oh, mi hijo. What am I going to do with you? You just said it again. I did not raise you that way; you are hopeless." She turned and plopped a steaming bowl of chili in front of me with a spoon and some freshly made warm tortillas. "Eat your beans and chili while I go start the laundry. We can talk more when you are finished."

I dug into the thick, aromatic chili, my spoon in one hand and my tortilla rolled up in the other, spooning and dipping, spooning and dipping, my senses wrapped around my taste buds. There was no better chili and beans than my mamacita's, absolutely none better. But then I could not be objective around her chili.

If you are of the Mexican culture you know that making chili is really an art form with recipes passed from generation to generation. And each family's chili recipe is like a personal signature. The chili has to be prepared with just the right amount of water, and simmered to a perfect consistency that is not too runny or too thick. Mama's chili was made with New Mexico chilies from Española or Hatch, spiced with plenty of garlic and other select ingredients, laced with pieces of diced or shredded pork meat. Since nothing was ever wasted in our house, Mama threw in the pork bones after they had been stripped of their meat saying that the bones enhanced the flavor. She would strip red chili pods from a ristra, or string, of red chilies that hung outside in the shade of the house, and then she would grind them to a powder using her old metate, a grinding bowl made of stone or fired clay. If making green chili she would use frozen green (verde) chilies that we would roast and peel when fresh was unavailable. Ahh, yes, chili verde. Loved it! We used chili verde with our beans, on sandwiches, on everything.

I vividly recall each fall after the harvest mi papito (my father) or mi mamacita buying freshly harvested chilies in fifty-pound gunnysacks. Then our families would gather around and roast and peel the chilies taking out the pods and seeds. My father liked his chili very hot and only had to warn us once about how the chilies could burn the skin if you were not careful in handling them. I learned this the hard way when I did not wash my hands before I went to the bathroom and had the unforgettable experience of burning my privates. After the roasting and peeling we would pack them in bags and freeze them to last, hopefully, through the winter until the next harvest.

Chili without beans? No way, Jose! Beans were another staple of life for Latinos and mi mamacita always had a pot of beans on the stove. And then there were her tortillas. To die for! She made her flour tortillas fresh every day. It was almost an art form watching her do her "tortilla magic."

First, she would make a bowlful of harina de masa (flour dough), scoop up a ball of dough from the bowl, and begin patting it in her hands. Next, she rolled it out with her old tried and true rolling pin. Her last step would be to toss it in the air, ending up with a magnificent tortilla that was almost perfectly round and just the right thickness. Trying this procedure myself just results in a tortilla mess on the floor. Lastly, she placed them into a hot pan, lifting and flipping them until they were perfectly roasted.

Tortillas, the Mexican equivalent of bread, also served another purpose as a superb eating utensil. With tortillas you don't always need a spoon since you can 'spoon' your beans and chili with the tortilla, or make the tortilla act as a 'bumper' to bump your food onto your fork. Most times no spoon is needed; just fill your tortilla scoop with chili or beans or whatever and you are in nirvana, Mexican style. And of course, the tortilla assures there is no waste because you use the doughy wonder to sop up any trace of juice or gravy from your bowl. A meal without tortillas—you've got to be kidding!

I snapped out of my chili reverie when mom came back from the laundry room. "How is the chili, hijo?"

By this time I was sopping up the last of the chili with my third tortilla. "Great as always, Mom. You know, as I was sitting here eating your chili, I remembered when we were kids and how we all helped to harvest the chilies and what a feast we had at the end of harvest with your chili, beans, tortillas, and empanadas for dessert. Back then we really didn't have much in material things did we, Mom? Especially at Christmas. But I remember you always managed to make us happy and fill our bellies with good food. Do you remember how everyone would come over to our little house—the sisters, brothers, aunts and uncles, all the cousins and friends?

There were tubs of beer and papito. All the uncles and cousins would sit around playing cards and joking till the wee hours of the morning while you and the aunties were all cooking up a storm. I remember you all made enough to feed everyone three times over. And you made the world's best pozole and would laugh and shake your finger at Dad and my uncles when you caught them swearing. Then we all slept where we could find a space, on the floor or out in the warm night air with nothing but a blanket to keep us warm and the ground as our mattress. Those were such good times, Mom, yet we had so little money. How did you ever manage to make us all so happy no matter how little we had?"

She smiled at me, put the laundry basket down and looked intently out the window for a few moments. "You know, hijo, when you mention Christmas it makes me think of when I was a little girl in Aguilar." Aguilar was the tiny town in Colorado where she spent her childhood. "We never had any presents or even a tree."

She fell silent so I prodded her a little. "Mamacita, was it because you were so poor?"

She hesitated then replied softly, "I don't remember." Even as I asked the question I already knew the answer. I knew she remembered, but this was her way of coping, that things were the way they were because it was God's will and His reasons were His own. I asked her to share what she did remember.

"Well," she said, "Christmas for us was a traditional 'La Posada' event." She sat down across from me. "Your aunt Sally and I looked forward to going around from neighbor to neighbor eating the goodies they made and enjoying the festive decorations. We lived in a little house where your grandma did the best she could for us. We were very poor so all she could afford for us was a single funny-looking stocking that she made and hung in the room that was our living room, dining room, kitchen, and bedroom combined. She filled that stocking with love and whatever candied goodies she could buy from the pennies and nickels she saved from her job as a house cleaner and a maid. Sis and I would share the contents of that one stocking. It was the only present I ever remember receiving as a child."

I looked at my mother, her inner strength, wondering how she managed with all us kids and how she kept going after mi papito died. Family was everything to us and Mom was the hub of it all. She kept us together, and our Christmases, though poor in material things, were rich in family and food.

Not wanting the stories to stop, I asked for another bowl of chili. I was already full, but sensed that Mama was in a story-telling mood and I didn't want to miss an opportunity to get her talking. The story that came up was the day my dad had the fishing accident that cost him his eye. Mom never wanted to talk about it. I went for it anyway. "Mom, do you remember what happened when dad lost his eye?"

A sad expression crossed her face. "Oh, hijo, I don't like to talk about it. I was the one to blame and it is hard, even now, to think about it."

I reached out and gave her an abrazo (hug) and kissed her lightly on her cheek. "I know it must be hard, Mom, but it was an accident. How about if I told you the story as I remember it and you correct me if I get it wrong?"

She thought for a moment, sighed, folded her hands in her lap and said, "Okay, hijo, go ahead."

The story lit up in my memory. I was about five or six and it was a warm Fourth of July day. The family was having a nice time by a crystal clear stream near San Luis where Dad, Mom, and my uncles, Jose and Esteban, were fly-fishing. I remember how it seemed that Dad was testing his patience to the limit trying to teach Mom how to cast. As I sat there on the bank of the river watching them, I glanced to the green field next to the river and noticed a big brown cow chewing her cud and swishing her tail just staring at me with her big brown eyes.

That sent my little boy's mind off on a little jog to the cow we had back in the mountain behind Monument Lake. Dad would milk the cow early in the morning and bring the milk home in a big pail where the whole family scooped it as needed in little cups, drinking it while it was still warm. All except me, that is. As a little boy I became spoiled when I visited my Auntie's house in Trinidad where milk was delivered fresh every morning in glass bottles and I developed this stubborn idea that milk was gross when drunk directly from a cow and I refused to drink it from the bucket. Dad would yell at me, "Mi hijo, be a man. Drink your milk!" I would look away and tearfully tell mi papito that it was hot and from a cow and I could not drink it that way. Dad figured out that what I wanted was only store-bought milk in a glass bottle and he wasn't happy about my attitude.

I looked over at my mom who had a little sly grin on her face because she knew what was coming. "So you, mi mamacita, would appease me by secretly pouring the milk from the pail of fresh cow milk into an old milk bottle you saved just for me. You would let me have my little fantasy that I was drinking milk just like it was delivered in bottles in Trinidad and I drank it all down, didn't I?"

Mama nodded and I returned to the fishing story.

I remembered how the sun glistened on the river's ripples, making them sparkle and dance. Mom did not really like to fish but she was trying her darndest to pay attention to Dad's instructions. She would do anything to please him; his needs and ours came before hers, always.

I could still hear him encouraging her. "That's it, Stella, let out a little more line. Gently now. That's better. Now watch me and see how I do it." He would demonstrate again, casting his own fly in rhythmic patterns allowing it to land gently onto surface of the water. Dad was an excellent trout fisherman. "See, Stella, see how it is done? Do it just like that."

Mom watched him intently and then said, "Okay, C, I think I can do it, but please let this be my last time because I need to go make us some lunch."

Mom raised her arm trying to mimic Dad and whipped the rod back and forth until the line made a sharp snapping sound. All hell broke loose. Dad screamed and staggered back onto the bank holding his hand over his eye. "Oh, God! Oh, Jesus Christ, Stella, you hooked me in the eye!" Mom's face turned grim as I related my recollection of the story but she did not stop me.

Mom dropped her fishing rod and ran back up the bank towards Papito. I can still hear her screaming, "Oh Celio, oh God! What have I done?!" Then she called for Uncle Jose and Esteben to help.

By the time they ran over to us Mom had tears rolling down her cheeks. Uncle Jose tried to gently work the hook out of dad's eye but with no success. By this time Dad's face had turned pasty white and his jaw was clenched tight in obvious pain. Finally, Uncle Jose asked Mom to lift his eyelid and hold his head steady while he did the only thing left to do. Then he quickly yanked the hook out taking some of the eye along with it. At that point mi poor papito groaned, jerked once and passed out.

Because of the long holiday weekend, we could not locate a doctor in the small town of San Luis where we staying at my aunt's house. Dad just laid there half in and half out of consciousness. I was scared out of my mind thinking my dad was dying but Mom kept telling me he was just resting his eye.

I looked over at Mom. "I remember that you finally found a doctor who said he needed to go to the hospital in Trinidad. We made the trek there and the next day they removed what was left of Dad's eye. While he was healing he wore a black patch over his eye while waiting for a glass eye to be made in Denver. I used to look at him, mesmerized by that patch, and fantasized that he looked just like a swashbuckling pirate.

"On one of our visits you bought Bobby and me some bubble gum. When we got to Dad's room everyone was making small talk and I had this great idea. I slipped out of the room and made myself a bubblegum eye patch. I strutted back in with this pink gooey mess plastered over my eye and eyebrow. Dad took one look at me and busted out laughing." Mom allowed herself a little smile in my direction.

"From his hospital bed, Dad said, 'Stella, you better tend to this boy's eye patch.'" I glanced sideways at my mom to guess her mood. "You did not see the humor in it when you spent over an hour trying to get it off. It was like glue, pulling out my eyelashes and little pieces of my eyebrow. You scolded me and asked me why I would do such a foolish thing. I started crying and told you I wanted to look just like Papito. Then you started crying and hugged me and weren't angry anymore."

Across the table from me, my mom gazed at me without blinking. "Yes, mi hijo, I think you have remembered the story very well and we don't have to speak of it again, okay?"

"Okay, Mamacita, and thank you for the beans and chili. I really have to go now but I promise to come back very soon and not wait so long." I held up three fingers, she laughed, and held up two and pushed me out the door.

I felt good when I left my mom's house that day, satiated with good food, stories, and righteously self-assured that all was well in my world and in hers. It would be the last time for a very long time that I would feel that way.

Not long after that visit, I called Lee to see if she had heard anything about mom's knee. Was it a simple cyst or a boil or infected splinter—what?

Lee hesitated then blurted, "It's cancer, Danny."

"Lee, you're kidding me, right? I saw the thing and felt it; it's just a little bump. Come on. There must be some kind of mistake."

"Trust me, Danny, it's no mistake. I wish it was. It is definitely cancer and a bone scan shows it has spread to other parts of her body. It's very serious. There is the option of multiple surgeries to buy some time, and of course, there's chemo and radiation. You and I need to talk about the best way to approach Mama and help her decide what to do."

It was as if someone had sucked the air out of my lungs and for a moment I could not speak, let alone take in what I was hearing. Mi Dios!

"Are you still there, Dan?" My sister's voice rose a notch. "Did you hear what I said?"

"Yeah, Lee, I heard you. I agree with you: We need to have a meeting to discuss this." I spoke with more confidence and authority than I felt. In fact, confidence had left me. I was alone and in shock.

I remember replaying my early conversations with Lee and my mother over and over in my head, berating myself for casually dismissing symptoms that would ultimately end my mother's life within eighteen months after the initial diagnosis. Like my mother's guilt over the incident with the fishing hook that cost my dad his eye, I buried my own self-proclaimed guilt deep within me where I would not have to deal with it, at least not for the moment. I would handle it later, I said to myself, much, much later.

We all wanted to spare Mom any unnecessary trauma so we downplayed it as much as possible while indicating that this was, in fact, serious, and that she needed to make some choices about treatment. Mom seemed to know her own mind. Looking at all the options, she chose to forego the surgeries because there were no guarantees of anything other than long and painful hospital stays, and she definitely did not want the debilitating effects that accompanied chemotherapy. She did agree to radiation in hopes of shrinking the tumors that were spreading. Unfortunately, after many months of radiation, it became apparent to the doctors that the cancer was spreading far more rapidly than we had anticipated and it was time to think about the next step, hospice care, to make her final months as comfortable as possible.

My sister Lee and other members of our family had had conversations over the years about what we would do when

Mom became incapacitated due to age. As custom and part of our heritage, we kept our elderly with us as part of the family and did not warehouse them in nursing homes. Talking about it was one thing, though; the reality of it was something else. Mom made it clear that she wanted to remain in her own home. I went through the motions of supporting my sister and agreeing that we would take care of her doing whatever was necessary to keep her in her home. I said all the right things, but secretly hoped my sister would figure out a way with the rest of the family to take care of it.

"So, how are we going to handle this?" I asked Lee during one of our meetings. "It doesn't seem like such a big deal."

Lee's temper flared, and rightfully so. "It IS a big deal, Dan, but how would you know since you have never taken care of anybody, especially Mama!"

My own guilt and denial made me defensive. "Oh yeah, Sis, just what do you mean by that?"

Lee backed off a bit. "Look Dan, there is no point in arguing about this now and we don't want to upset Mom. We are going to need each other to get through this."

Lee's training as a nurse gave her an advantage and she knew what was coming down the pike. I took a good look at her and noticed for the first time how tired she looked. The third oldest in our family, Lee was the one always in control, the one who came up with a plan during a crisis. But even my levelheaded sister had no magic formula about how this would play out. Our mother was dying. That was our certainty.

Getting a grip on her anxiety, Lee went on. "Look, Mom's okay for now. She's got some pain, but I worry about what's going to happen when she really starts to suffer—you know, when she, uh, starts to die."

Once again I piped up inserting my insensitive two cents worth. "Come on, Sis, she's already starting to die. We'll just handle it."

I have to give my sister credit for not hitting me in the head with something large and lethal. Although her eyes revealed shock at my stupid comment, she responded as calmly as possible. "Oh, Dan, sometimes I think you are so clueless. You don't know anything about these things." She sighed. "No matter what, we will work through it together."

Seeing the pain and frustration on my sister's face I relented. "Okay, Sis, I'll admit I'm no expert on this subject, so what do you propose we do?"

She thought for a moment. "I believe that one of us may know someone at hospice who helps families care for their terminally ill. I'll see if I can find out more information."

It was an idea, the beginnings of a plan that did not immediately involve me, and I jumped on it. "Yeah, Lee, that sounds like a good idea. When I was on city council I voted to provide funds for hospice and I was really impressed with their program. Call when you find out something."

That macho Latino male part of me asserted that it was the woman's job to take care of the sick and ailing, wasn't it? Even as I thought these things I found myself once again in denial, stuffing those shameful feelings deep within, adding to the guilt that was already there. I wondered vaguely how much my mind and body would hold before it burst from the sheer volume of it.

Chapter 2

"We are healed of suffering only by
expressing it to the full."

Marcel Proust

"Danny, this is Lee. Can you meet me at hospice at nine
Tuesday morning? It's a little two story white house located
west of the church on Ninth Ave."
"Yeah, I know where it is. I used to attend rotary meetings
at the church next door. So what's this about?" It was a stupid
question, but my denial was well in place by this time. And if
I did not talk about it or think about it, maybe it would all just
go away on its own. I could almost see my sister roll her eyes
at me over the phone.
"They're going to talk to us about what we can expect
with Mom's cancer and how they can help us with her care."
So now I was back to something I definitely was not
comfortable with: reality and taking care of Mom. "Lee, are
you sure this is not something I can talk to them about on
the phone?"
"Come on, Danny. You can make the time. This is
about Mom and you promised you would be part of this. I
don't know what they're going to tell us, but we need to be
there, okay?"
I was familiar with the little house on Ninth Avenue. I
had been there many times over the past few years for social
service events as part of programs I supported when I was on
the city council.

When we arrived we were greeted warmly by one of the hospice staff members, Sheila. "Aren't you Dan Benavidez? Weren't you on the City Council? I used to see you on television for the city council meetings and I just want to thank you for all you've done in support of our programs."

I gave her one of my most self-assured and, I thought, winning smiles. "Well thank you, and yes, that would be me. I never dreamed that I would be here asking for YOUR support." Stay in control, Dan, I told myself. Just stay in control.

Sheila touched my arm briefly. "Yes, life is strange that way. We never know in advance what's in store for us, and perhaps that is a good thing. What do you say we sit down and get started?" She led us into a small private room and began, what I figured, was the standard speech about death and dying. I plastered the "I'm interested" look on my face and tried not to glance at my watch.

"Taking care of someone who is dying is far from easy," Sheila began. "It's even more difficult when it's someone as close to you as your mother. We are here to support you and your mother throughout the whole process. We will handle the medications she may need and you can administer them yourselves, whenever appropriate, if that is your choice. We will be there by your side, working inside and outside of your mother's home, and are available to you at any time of the day or night should you need us, either with a concern about your mother or just to talk. Do you understand?"

Lee acknowledged that she did and I vaguely remember nodding my head in Sheila's general direction.

Sheila went on, her voice soft and droning in my ears. "I'm going to give you this booklet that will explain in some detail the kinds of things you and your mother can expect over the next few months. It will help you recognize and understand the signs of Stella's eventual decline as the cancer escalates and she moves closer to her transition."

I thought to myself, *Transition? That means death, right?* Sheila's voice became a distant hum and I drifted away from the conversation. My body stayed where it was because it could not move, but my mind went into escape mode. I remember feeling very uncomfortable and my mood turned foul. Why the hell was I here? I didn't need any booklet or anyone telling me when or how my mom is going to die. Besides, it should be pretty damned obvious when it happens, and my sister Lee will be there, woman to woman, as it should be. Of course, she may think she needs me as the big brother and I will do my part. I mean, how complicated could it be?

I was suddenly aware that it felt warm and stuffy in that small office. Couldn't they get some air in there? I took a sip of my now cold, instant coffee and it tasted bitter. I glanced around at the walls and noticed all the posters with touchy-feely sentiments and pictures meant to inspire. Even Sheila had this same touchy-feely attitude and it grated on me. I told myself to calm down, asking myself, What am I missing here that seems to have the full attention of my sister? I did not need consoling or little "goody" hugs or light kisses on my cheek. I certainly felt no need to share my feelings with a complete stranger, let alone with my sister. I felt that Lee could handle all that mushy stuff and do the crying when it was necessary and I would be the strong, silent brother who holds it all together. And I reminded myself that Sheila was just doing her job and the least I could do was look interested.

Looking back, the wisdom and experience, not to mention the patience, of Sheila and her coworkers at hospice were truly amazing. She probably knew more about who I was, especially the piece of me that I was carefully concealing, than I did at the time. I came out of my reverie and mind-talk to find everyone, especially Sheila, looking at me.

She asked, "Dan, how do you feel about all of this so far?" In my mind I wanted to shout, "Well shit, how in the hell do you think I feel about this?" I knew if I did not get out of there soon I would either start yelling at someone or be violently ill.

With my fake smile still plastered on my face, I got up, leaned over the desk, and firmly shook Sheila's hand, speaking confidently and not a little abruptly: "Well, it all looks good to me, and if I need any help I'll be sure to call you. But right now I really need to get back to my office."

Sheila released my hand, but held me captive with her eyes. "Okay, Dan. I do understand that you are very busy, but please remember that hospice is here to help families such as yours. And we want to help you honor your mother's wishes to remain in her own home surrounded by her loved ones. This will not be an easy task for any of you and, most importantly, we want to be sure you understand, really understand, that this is a partnership between us. In this way your mother's remaining days will be as comfortable and happy as possible —for all of you."

I bobbed my head up and down as I moved toward the door. "Yeah, thanks again, Sheila, and we will look at everything you gave us."

"Not a problem, Dan, and thanks for making the time to meet with me. I know this is a huge and difficult decision and my prayers go with you."

Smiling my best councilman smile, I left with Lee following, and we walked outside. I took great gulps of air, feeling like I had been deprived of oxygen.

Lee stopped me before I could get to my car. "Danny, let's get a cup of coffee and discuss this."

I had almost escaped. My voice took on a hard edge as I rounded on my sister. "Look, Lee, it isn't necessary, and we know what we have to do. We already talked about how much Mom needs us and we need her and all that stuff about family. *I know, I know.* Why do we have to keep going over this?"

Lee could tell I was on the verge of something disastrous and wisely backed off. "You're right, Dan, we can take a rain check on coffee and talk later, okay?"

"Yeah. You take care, okay? And I want you to know that I understand this is about familia and I promise we are in it together." I tried to sound more supportive than I felt. "Say, do you know if Mom knows yet that her cancer is terminal? I mean, that she has only a short time left?" Lee shook her head and looked at me expectantly. Okay, I got it: She wanted me to step up to the plate. "How about I drop by Mom's house and see if I can detect how much she knows, and I will call you later?" Somewhat relieved, my sister agreed and I finally escaped to the safety of my car.

I didn't realize until I pulled out my car keys that my hands were shaking and my palms were slick with sweat. I had done a great job up to now acting like a great, successful Mexican-American in a white man's community, showing people how motivated and strong I was. I was getting a small inkling that some dark beast was awakening deep inside me and I was about to begin a journey that could very well bring me to my knees and blow apart the life I had so carefully constructed. Something else hovered just inside my consciousness and I gripped the wheel so tightly my knuckles ached. My stomach turned to acid and that unknown beast rose like bile up my throat. It had a name: Fear.

Back at Mom's I hesitated, calling out to her before I entered. "Hey, Mom, it's me, Danny."

"Danny, come in, silly," she replied. "You don't need to holler at the door. You are just in time for some dinner. Sit down and have some good food. I don't know how you can live on all the junk you eat."

I sat down and grabbed the warm tortilla, digging into my chili without saying much, which was unusual for me. I even forgot the finger game.

Mom stood next to me for a moment watching me eat. "What are you thinking, Danny?"

"Nothing, Mom. Just how good the beans and chili are, as always." I met her gaze briefly and dove back into my chili.

"Ah, hijo, I can see something bothers you. Tell me, is it about me, about my dying?"

I nearly choked on the chili and found myself sweating, beads of it running off my brow.

Mama looked alarmed. "Danny, you are sweating? Is the chili too hot?"

My hand shook and I spilled chili down the front of my shirt. My eyes welled up with tears that I could not stop and they ran down my cheeks. My mother sat down and put her hand on my arm to stop the trembling. "Ah, mi hijo, don't cry. I know I am going to die soon and it is okay. God wants me to come home and be with Daddy."

Suddenly, I was a little boy again, pouring out his heart to his mamacita, and feeling ashamed that this frail, dying woman was a stronger spirit than I. "Oh, Mama, I do love you. You are being so kind to me and I know I have not been such a good son."

"Mi hijo, what is this all about? I am very proud of you and all the things you have done. I have all the newspaper clippings and I show them to everybody."

I was not about to be consoled. "But Mama, you don't know I spent most of my time satisfying my own ego and not being around more for you or my family. I even resented the smallest chores you asked me to do as if it was beneath me to do them. You thought I was good, but I was weak. I am so sorry."

My mother tightened her grip on my arm. "Listen, hijo, you were always here when I truly needed you. I know you have your own life. As far as I am concerned, I raised a fine son and that is good enough for me."

The bottom line was my mother knew she was dying and was prepared for it. Now she had to prepare me. Me, me, me; again I made it all about me. Once again I stuffed another shameful piece of baggage into my already overstuffed inner closet for another day.

It would be a long time before I would allow myself to see and fully appreciate the flaming colors of a Colorado sunset, something I have always loved. My once-colorful world turned into several shades of gray and sleepless nights became the norm. I would pray for sleep that was peaceful and without interruption, either from Mama's physical needs or my raging inner demons, the latter being the worst and most difficult to soothe.

Lee worked out a rotating shift defining who would spend which nights with Mom. She was amazing. She even had the schedule and instructions for administering all her meds and personal needs, such as bathing and making sure Mom was moved properly into various positions to keep bed sores to a minimum. All this involved me, Lee, her husband Ted, and other members of the family who would pitch in as they could to relieve us. My brother Bobby and his wife Dolores lived in New Mexico and came up whenever they could, as well as numerous cousins and friends. People were coming and going at all hours of the day and night and at times it seemed like a mad house. It took me a long time to recognize and fully appreciate the love and support we had from everyone. I guess I was too knee-deep in my own alligators to see much of anything at the time.

Those early weeks with Mom were all part of a dance of preparation. She could still do for herself, but it was obvious she was weakening, and with the increasing pain she needed someone to be there during the days to make sure she ate, took her meds on time, and did not fall. I was mainly day-shift at this point. Sometimes Mom cooked and sometimes I cooked, although when I cooked she spent the whole time telling me what I was doing wrong.

I wasn't sure whether she was preparing herself or me, but our conversations were sometimes strained with both of us trying to be lighthearted for the other and neither of us succeeding very well. Out of the blue my mother would say, "You know, hijo, I am ready to go see God, but I don't know how I will handle not having you with me." Rather than being quiet and recognize her need to talk, I'd make a flippant remark I regretted the moment the words left my lips: "Hey, Mom, the way things are going in my life right now I'll probably beat you there."

"Oh, hijo, don't talk like that. I could not bear it if one of you children should go before me."

I could have bitten my tongue off. She was dying, knew it, and yet I had upset her needlessly with a careless remark. All I could stammer was, "My God, Mom, your days are numbered yet you still think of all of us first. You should be thinking of yourself and telling us what you need."

Mom continued to assure me that she really was prepared to "go meet Daddy," but I could see that her eyes did not match the words. Her eyes reflected what I felt at the core of my being—terror. How do I help her when I cannot help myself? What can I say to divert her attention and mine from the topic of death?

I suddenly smiled and grabbed her hand. "Mom, do you remember how Bobby and I used to make money from catching fish and selling them to the gringos from Trinidad and Denver?"

Jumping on the diversion, she leaned forward. "Oh, yes, that is a funny story. Tell me again."

We lived at the time in the mountains in southern Colorado. A half-mile from our house was a private gate to our property just over a quaint, wooden bridge. The crystal clear stream flowing under this bridge was noted for good trout fishing, if you knew where to find them. And we knew all the best trout hiding places. With the spring run-off the stream was full and moving swiftly over the rocks and Bobby and I were tromping up and down the banks.

Suddenly we heard voices up by the bridge. Three Anglos were trying to get in the gate. When they saw us down below they hollered at us. "Hey, little boys, can we come in and fish? We haven't had much luck downstream."

Bobby looked at me and whispered, "We better not say yes until we ask Dad. You tell them, okay?" He tried to shove me forward.

"Hey, Bobby, why do I have to be the one to tell them? You tell them!"

Bobby fixed me with the "big brother" look. "Because I'm older than you. Now do it."

I took a few steps up the bank and tried to make my voice sound important while not actually making eye contact. "Gee, mister, we can't let you in till we get permission from our dad and we don't know where he is right now." I turned around hoping this would be the end of it and they would leave, but one of the voices stopped me.

"Listen, kid, we haven't had any luck and we don't want to go home all skunked with no catch, so whatta ya say to a half-dollar each if you let us in?"

My eyes went wide as I turned to Bobby and whispered, "A whole dollar, Bobby. That's a bunch of money."

Bobby grabbed my arm. "Yeah, I know, but we can't let them in without Dad's permission. But you can tell them that if they wait here for half an hour we can go upstream and catch some nice big trout for them to take home."

I did as I was told and two of the fishermen shook their heads in agreement. The fattest of the Anglos, though, looked me in the eye and said, "Okay, but you don't get paid till you bring us the fish and they better be good ones."

We nodded our heads vigorously. I spoke in my most authoritative voice. "You bet, mister. We'll catch real big ones."

We stared open-mouthed as the three made themselves comfortable on the grass, opening their knapsacks and pulling out several bottles of beer, popping off the tops, and throwing them in the grass. The fat Anglo saw us still standing there and shouted, "Well, what are you waiting for? Get on with it!"

With the thought of that dollar in our heads, we raced home, got our willow poles, safety pins, dug up some worms in the bare, moist spot next to the house, and off we went to our "secret" fishing spot. Bobby caught the first one and had to jump in to wrestle it with his hands because it was big enough that our safety pins might not hold up under the strain. He even went under a couple of times hanging onto his pole and easing the fighting fish to him. After about five minutes he popped up holding a whopper, a smile plastered to his face.

"Wow, Danny, they will really like this one! They might even give us more money." We both began to fish in earnest and in a very short time had bagged a dozen nice rainbows and two German browns all twelve to seventeen inches long. Proud of our catch, we headed back to the waiting Anglos. Bobby turned to me with light in his eyes. "Danny, why don't you ask them for more money since these are real beauties and they would never have found our secret spot?"

I stopped in my tracks. "It was your idea, Bobby. You ask them. It's not fair I have to do it."

Once again the old argument ensued. "I told you, Danny: I'm older than you and I know more than you do."

I pouted. "Okay, I'll do it, but I'm telling Mom that you always make me do everything just 'cause you don't want to."

We found the men laughing and content on the grass, empty beer bottles strewn around them. We ran up the bank and through the gate. Bobby pushed me forward. "Mister, sir, we, ah, got you some real nice trout, and big and, uh, can we have our money now?"

Mr. Fat Man glared down at me. "Show me the fish first, kid."

Bobby and I spread our precious catch on the grass for the men to see. The men smiled at each other.

"Jesus, these are real beauties. Here's your dollar." He handed the bill to Bobby, who managed to look at it and mumble, "Uh, mister, sir, do you think that maybe this many big trout are worth a little more than a dollar?"

I was proud of my brother in that moment for speaking up to this nasty looking Anglo. My little bubble of hope burst, though, when Mr. Fat Man replied with a smirk, "Shit no, a deal's a deal. Besides, you kids won't even know what to do with this much money anyway." The three men thought this last remark pretty funny and seemed a little tipsy as they bent to gather up their stuff. They grabbed up the fish and staggered off down the road to their car, leaving the empty beer bottles on the grass.

On the way home I reached for the dollar. "Bobby, can I hold it?"

Bobby snatched his hand away. "No, I'll hold it."

I whined at him. "But why do you always get to keep things?"

"Because I'm older. I already told you: The older one gets more." Bobby kept walking.

"Pleeeeease let me hold it, please, Bobby? It's half mine." I grabbed his arm, which was not a good idea.

Bobby shook me off. "Let go of me. Besides, I have to figure out what to do with this money. And I don't think you deserve half because I caught more fish than you did."

I was getting mad and pulled out my ace in the hole. "You better give me half or I'm telling Mom. And I think we should tell Mom what happened anyway."

Bobby finally relented. "Ahhhhh, okay, don't get excited. We'll tell her. Now leave me alone."

"Mama, Mama, look what we got! We're rich!" Bobby waved the dollar over his head as he raced first into the house.

Mom turned around and eyed my brother standing there dripping all over the floor. "Bobby, why are your clothes and hair all wet? Didn't I tell you to stay out of the river when it's high? You could drown."

Bobby waved the dollar in her face. She narrowed her eyes at us. "Bobby, where did you get that?"

Bobby grinned. "We earned it, Mama. Some gringos gave it to us for catching fish down by the gate."

Mama looked unconvinced. "Now don't lie to me. Nobody would pay you boys for fish."

I chimed in, dancing in front of Bobby. "But they did, Mama, they really did, and now Bobby won't give me my share and it's not fair. Make him give me my share."

Our mother sighed. "You boys better sit down and tell me the whole story."

As we recounted the story, our mother slowly broke into a smile. "Are you sure these men actually paid you for the fish?"

We bobbed our heads up and down. "Yes, yes, they really did, a whole dollar."

Although she was still smiling, she shook her finger at us. "Well, that was very nice, boys, but you know you really should have just given the fish to those men. It is not really right that people should pay to fish here, even gringos." Then to our surprise she reached out and hugged us both.

We asked hopefully, "Does that mean we can keep the dollar, mama?"

"Okay, but just this once, mi hijos. Give the dollar to me and when I go to town I will buy each of you some bubble gum, and if there is a little left over some flour for tortillas, okay?"

We thought that sounded great. As Bobby went off to change his wet clothes Mama called out to him. "Promise me you won't go back into that river when it is high, okay? And another thing, if you meet anyone else who wants fish, you let them have it for free because that is the nice thing to do. And, Bobby, it is not right that you would not share with your brother."

Bobby hung his head, but only for a moment, and then raced off to change his clothes with me hard on his heels, both of us so excited we forgot our argument.

By ourselves and with our own ingenuity, we earned a whole dollar that would be used to buy flour for food and bubble gum for each of us. Better than that, we knew Mama was secretly proud because she smiled and hugged us. Life was good that day.

Chapter 3

"Nobody realizes that some people
expend tremendous energy merely to be normal."

Albert Camus

We dubbed it "The Blue Beast." Specially designed for the particular needs of those in declining health and mobility, the chair was lent to us by hospice. It was completely motorized with a tilting back and adjustable arms and legs that we learned to manipulate and maneuver to within a millimeter of comfort. Often that millimeter made all the difference to the pain registered on Mom's face. It is amazing how a large inanimate object, such as a big blue recliner chair, took on a personality of its own becoming the focal point of my mother's final months. It was her throne and her Alamo. From "the Blue Beast" she courageously fought the disease that moved with a raging impartiality through her body. Sitting in the middle of the living room my mother, Queen of the Recliner, lived out most of her remaining months. She slept, took her meals, received massages, and all her personal and intimate body care from that chair. One of us would sleep nearby, usually on the couch, to be accessible if she needed something in the night.

All life pulsed around the Beast, with which I had a love-hate relationship. I hated it because it seemed nothing more than a rolling hearse with a living body still in it. I loved it when I was able to manipulate its many positions to one that allowed her to sigh in temporary relief and comfort. Then I would hold her hand until she drifted off to sleep. How many nights did we do that? I lost count. When the chair did not cooperate and she struggled to find a comfortable position, we told stories to distract her from the pain. Soon, the memories of the past became a blur that mingled with the present as those stories sustained us and kept reality at bay.

One night we were waging a battle with the Beast. None of its hundred positions or several pillows was working and both Mom and I were becoming frustrated.

"Son, could you move the little one under my arm a little bit more?" Her voice, though filled with pain, was patient.

"Damn, Mom, I've moved every lever and every pillow in all directions and it never seems to do any good!" I, of course, had no patience.

"I know, son, you are doing your best, but please don't use bad language, okay?" I clenched my jaw and went at it again. "Oh, that's a little better, son. Now just a bit more to the right." She was trying so hard to be helpful while I was thinking all about, you guessed it, me. My fear had turned to a deep and simmering anger some time before and, without being conscious of it, I was taking it out on Mom.

"Okay, okay. Give me a break, Mom. I'm doing the best I can."

I'm not sure whether my mother actually found a comfortable position or whether she was just trying to placate me, but I suspect the latter. She finally indicated that she was fine and I was all too willing to believe her.

"It's okay, hijo," she reassured me. "You are doing fine and don't worry. Lolly will be here soon and she knows how to do it. Just don't get upset, okay?" The kinder she was the more I loathed myself for my insensitivity, my intolerance, and my ineptitude towards my mother's care. She was dying by bits and pieces and I was completely and totally helpless to change that—not something I could easily come to terms with. And certainly not for a man who prided himself on control.

Just when I thought I was getting a handle on the Beast and the pillows, the bedsores arrived with a vengeance. Lolly and Aja would work together, gently raising her nightshirt while Ted and I turned her over. Then the girls would rub salve on the angry open sores on her back and buttocks. I swallowed hard and turned my head away from the vision of that poor little body festered with open sores and swollen with cancer. So much for macho, Dan. I'd take a gang fight any day over this.

Going to the bathroom was a major undertaking, especially when she broke her hip and could no longer make it there by herself. She refused a bedpan because, in her mind, that was her last straw in hanging onto some small shred of independence and dignity, and God knows, she had very little left. At first it took twenty minutes for me to help her to the bathroom. Men just didn't do this stuff, you know? When I was alone with her and had to do the bathroom ritual I would curse under my breath about what a pain in the ass this was with all the mess to clean up. (Just writing this puts a knot in my stomach, not about the mess, but about my attitude.) I was resistant to the opportunity for learning before me that made the process doubly painful for everyone concerned.

Mom, hearing my cursing, pleaded with me, tears streaking her cheeks. "I know this is hard on you, son, and I am sorry. But please have a little patience with me, please!" I remember muttering a quick apology with not a lot of feeling in it. I gritted my teeth, holding on to her from behind, and walked the long mile to the toilet, turning her and holding her clothes and hands as she lowered herself. I remained there steadying her while she went about her "business," cleaning her up after. This is the most private of a human's personal hygiene and it tore any last piece of dignity away from this woman who was my mother and further fueled my building rage against just about everybody, including God.

Sometimes these "potty breaks" took quite some time, and to take both our minds off the obvious, I would tell a story. "You know, Mom, Bobby and I were talking on the phone yesterday and he asked me to ask you if you remember the time when we were little, living on the ranch and we borrowed Daddy's tractor?" Mom got a little smile on her face and nodded, looking up at me expectantly. I concentrated my gaze on the wall above my mother's head, giving us both a pitiful illusion of privacy, as I recalled the story.

Bobby and I had been sitting around doing what we did best, which was nothing, when I suddenly had one of my brilliant ideas. "You know, Bobby, I bet it would really help Dad if we could plow the field for him. I heard him talking to Mom about how busy he is cutting up logs with Mr. Duran and he doesn't have time to get the field ready for planting."

Bobby looked down, shuffling the dirt with his foot. "I don't know about that, Dan. Dad's funny about that tractor."

"Yeah, Bobby, I know, but I've seen him do it lots and it looks pretty easy if we do it together. Whaddya say?" I could tell Bobby was thinking about it.

"Hmmmm. Well, it might work because I've watched him, too. I just have to figure out how to get it started, and then I think I can drive it if you work the plow."

We raced down to the field where Dad kept the tractor, all excited about this new adventure and surprising Dad with a freshly plowed field. I hopped up on the tractor with Bobby close behind.

"Okay, Bobby, I'll sit back here on the plow and work this lever up and down. I think that's how it works."

My brother was fiddling with the pedals and things. "All right, let's do it. This must be the starter pedal. Maybe if I push . . ."

"Careful, Bobby. You sure you know what you're doing?"

"Shut up. There's really nothing to it. You're always worrying about stuff. See, I'm just gonna turn on this switch and mash the pedal on the floor like Dad does."

The engine emitted a low growl and then went dead. I sat back on the plow, waiting for Bobby to do his thing and we could get going. "Anything wrong, Bobby?"

"Nope. I told you to not to worry, so quit bugging me."

Bobby was getting frustrated. After what seemed like an eternity, Bobby again mashed his foot down on the starter pedal. The engine growled and he let out the clutch, and this time we were rewarded with a small forward lurch before it stopped. I got excited. "Hey, Bobby, I think it moved!"

"Yeah, Danny, I know. I think I got it now." And with that he mashed his foot down on the starter pedal one more time and when he let out the clutch the tractor gave a violent pitch forward before hiccupping to a stop.

"Do it again, Bobby, hurry!" The instant Bobby's foot hit the starter pedal the engine erupted with a loud bang, belched out a puff of black smoke and came to life with a low thump, thump, thump. As he let out the clutch, it chugged forward.

"Wahoo! All right, Bobby! We're moving!"

Bobby had a smug look on his face. "Hey, bro, I told you there was nothing to it, didn't I?"

Our boyish high was short-lived when the engine suddenly gave a mighty cough and erupted fully to life. It accelerated from a manageable crawl to a speed immediately terrifying to two young brothers.

"What's happening, Bob? We're going pretty fast. Are we okay?" I was holding on to keep from falling off.

Bobby was sweating and his eyes looked really huge. "I'm not sure. Maybe it has something to do with how I work the pedals on the floor. Daddy talked about working the clutch a certain way." Bobby frantically tried working the pedal but the tractor was definitely out of control.

My voice was a high-pitched screech. "Do something! We're heading toward the creek!"

My brother didn't answer. He was hanging onto the steering wheel trying to turn it, but he wasn't strong enough.

He swung around to me, fear all over his face. "Jump, Danny, jump! Now! Hurry! Get off! Get off! I can't stop it!"

I flung myself off the tractor, hitting the ground hard and tumbling over and over landing in the mud on my back. When I looked up I saw Bobby still hanging on, screaming, "Oh God, oh God, Mama, Mama!" At the last minute he vaulted off the tractor landing first on his feet, then tripping and tumbling head over heels down the hill right behind the tractor. I ran after him sobbing. "Look at it go, Bob! Stop it! Do something!"

Bobby got up, turned on me and shouted, "Me, I can't do anything. I don't know how! You're the one who said you knew what to do. This was your idea, not mine!"

We collapsed in the grass and watched helplessly as the tractor gathered speed, belching and thumping faster and faster until it reached the creek. We stared in awe as the tractor crashed right into the creek and kept right on going to the other side where it smashed into a cottonwood nose first, roaring and belching like a mighty volcano, its wheels spinning and churning up mud. Finally, with a last puff of black smoke and steam the engine died and the tractor slumped, its front tires hopelessly tangled in the low-hanging branches of the cottonwood.

An eerie quiet settled over us. There was a slight smell of fuel and the creek bubbled on like before. Other than a few scratches and a lot of dirt we were not hurt. My brother's voice was barely a whisper. "Dad's gonna kill us." Then he looked right at me, fear turned to anger. "Boy oh boy, Danny, you really did it this time."

I cried even harder. "Not *me*, Bobby. It's not my fault. I'm gonna tell Daddy it was *you* who started the tractor and you said you knew how to drive it, not me."

Hearing all the screaming and commotion, our mother came over the hill to see what was going on. When she saw Bobby and me sprawled in the grass covered in mud she panicked and ran towards us.

"Oh God, are you boys all right? Please, God, let them be all right!" She hovered over us, checking each of us out with her hands and eyes. Once she had wiped away some of the mud and was sure we were not hurt she sat back and took a good look at the tractor sitting on the other side of the creek. She folded her arms and waited. I started crying again and Bobby hung his head. She gathered us together and put her arms around us. "What were you boys thinking? Don't you have any sense at all? You are so lucky you were not hurt—or worse." She shuddered and hugged us close. She wasn't exactly yelling at us, so I got up enough courage to tell her our plan to help Dad. She smiled briefly, sighed, and put a serious look back on her face.

"A que mis hijos, oh my sons, I don't know what I am going to tell your Dad. I thank God you are all right and I will figure out something, but promise me you will *never* do that again. Never. Promise me."

Mom greeted my Dad as he came in the door. "C, did you have a good day?"

"No, not so good, Stella. We got the truck stuck up near Truchas and had to unload it to get it out. It took all day and we didn't get much done." Dad looked hot and tired and Bobby and I were trying to be invisible over in the corner.

My mom kept up the conversation. "Are you hungry?"

"Yeah, I could eat a horse. Let me clean up and relax a little before we eat, okay? I sure could use a little peace and quiet after such a rough day."

Mom smiled sweetly at Dad. "That's good, C. Maybe before you get all settled I should show you something down by the creek, okay?"

"Gee, Stella, I'm real tired. Can't it wait till after supper?" Dad started to head off to wash up.

"No, C, I'm afraid it can't. It's important and maybe you better come see for yourself, right now."

Now she had Dad's full attention. "See what, Stella? What are you talking about?"

She moved toward the door. "It's difficult to explain, C. It's best you see for yourself."

"Oh, all right, let's get it over with so we can come back and eat. Let's go."

Mom turned toward us and, with her back to Dad, made the sign of the cross. "Come on, boys, let's go." On wobbly legs we followed our parents down to the creek.

Dad just stood there, mouth hanging open, shaking his head in total disbelief at the sight of the tractor half-buried on the other side of the creek. "Stella, what in the hell happened?!"

"Now, C, try to stay calm. Don't be too harsh on the boys. They were just trying to help you." Mom stood next to Dad with Bobby and me on the other side of her out of Dad's swinging range. Then she told him our story.

A lot of emotions crossed our Dad's face but one of them was a grin that he quickly covered up with a cough. He stepped around our mother and towered over both of us. We were busy studying something on the ground by our feet, our chins tucked firmly into our chests.

His voice sliced the warm air and turned it cold. "Don't you *ever* do anything like that again, you hear? You touch anything without my permission and I'll take a strap to you. Look at me when I'm talking. Do you understand?"

We gulped and muttered something that indicated we understood and waited. Dad turned to Mom, winked at her and said, "Y'know, these boys are getting big enough to help out more around here, so maybe I'll just have to teach them how to drive that tractor all by themselves."

Mom smacked him on the arm and laughed. "Don't you dare, C. They're still just little boys."

Dad turned around letting us see his grin. "Well, maybe another year, but right now I'm really hungry. Let's go eat some of your mom's good beans and chili. I'll get the truck and me and Mr. Duran will haul that tractor out in the morning." Mom hugged Dad, then turned her back to him and mouthed the words, "Thank you, God."

Back home, we couldn't do enough for Dad. I ran and got Dad a cold beer while Bobby got him his slippers. He stretched out with a little grin on his face watching us, knowing full well how grateful two little boys were to be allowed to live, and that they would most likely get into mischief again some other day.

Mom finished her "business," was cleaned up and back in the arms of the Blue Beast. She looked at me. "I had almost forgotten that story, hijo. Your father really enjoyed watching you and your brother squirm." She laughed then. "You know, hijo, it wasn't too many months after that when Daddy packed everyone up and followed his brothers to Ely, Nevada, to work in the copper mines."

"Yeah, Ma, I remember." I shut my eyes remembering too much. Ely, Nevada, a copper mining town where we learned some of the people there disliked Mexicans AND Catholics and we just happened to be both. But that is another story for another time.

Chapter 4

"In the confrontation between the stream and the rock, the
stream always wins—not through strength but
by perseverance."

H. Jackson Brown

As the days and weeks ebbed and flowed I thought of the
low self -esteem that can be cultivated from being a minority
in a predominately white culture. Sometimes Mama's stories
brought back an unpleasant memory, like an old wound that
would not quite heal. I know what I had experienced personally
as a child and then as a young man in my community and I
wondered at what it must have been like in my mother's day
as a Hispanic in a white society. One of her stories brought
the point poignantly home because it led to a tragedy within
our own family.

Like me, my mother's cousin Jake Trujillo had a rough
time dealing with his Hispanic heritage. More than once Mom
heard him say, "I'd do anything if I could remove the Spanish
blood from my veins." Note he said Spanish not Mexican. It
wasn't much but Spanish was a step above Mexican on the
social acceptability scale. Personally, I think his bitterness
stemmed from his numerous confrontations in Aguilar,
experiences that he judged to be demeaning and blatantly
discriminatory.

Jake was having a torrid affair with an Anglo (white) girl
named Vietta. From what we could determine, they loved each
other very much but could not marry because it was socially

taboo for intermarriages between Anglos and Hispanics in Aguilar. They had to content themselves with clandestine meetings on the swinging bridge, a favorite spot for lovers. To add fuel to an already combustible situation, Vietta was coveted by a local Anglo man. This man was extremely jealous and spread the word around town that any white girl who valued her reputation should never be seen with a "damn Mexican." He of course hated Jake as passionately as Jake loved Vietta, and the tension building in that village was almost palpable as folks waited for something to snap. They didn't have to wait long.

One Sunday afternoon Jake and Vietta were together at the swinging bridge with their arms wrapped around each other when the Anglo found them. He had been trying to catch them for some time and now he confronted Jake on the bridge. Words got hot and gestures became aggressive between the two men while Vietta cried and implored them to stop. It was then the Anglo pulled out a gun and shot Jake point-blank right there on the bridge, killing him.

It took the family a long time to recover from that tragedy, more so because they felt so helpless. It was such a senseless thing and yet much of the community did not act surprised that it happened. After all, Jake and Vietta KNEW the social rules didn't they? There were some things you just didn't do and not suffer some sort of consequence. Unfortunately, killing a Mexican man was not one of them. Thinking on it much later, I figured it just might have done Jake some good if there had been a way for him to have a massive transfusion of Anglo blood, assuming they could also change his looks, name, and ancestry. As it was, some white man finally did relieve him of a large volume of the Mexican blood he hated so much, the hard way.

Aguilar was also my mother's place of birth and there were pleasant memories alongside the painful ones. Her first house was in downtown Aguilar near the A.I. Lindsey Lumber Mill. Mama told me of the wonderful times she and her sister

Sally had when they had just enough money to walk to Mr. Jamieson's grocery store to buy penny candy. Aunt Sally and Mama would take their time drooling over all the delicious candy in big glass jars and then point with their fingers to the ones they wanted, eyes wide with anticipation as the grocer put them in a little bag. Back then you took your grocery list to the store, handed your list to Mr. Jamieson, and he or his helper would go around the store, pulling everything needed off this shelf or that, putting the items in your basket for you.

On one particular day, Mama and Aunt Sally were on their way to the store talking about the candy they were going to buy when they spotted a paper package lying by the side of the road. It must have fallen off someone's wagon or bike. Curious, the girls opened the package and found two beautiful dresses, all frilly with lots of lace and bows. "Que milagro! (What a miracle!)," shouted Sally. They looked around and, seeing no one about, took the dresses home where they tried them on, turning this way and that, oohing and aahing at how beautiful they looked and how good they fit. They debated whether to go back to the store to see if anyone was missing a package.

"You know, Sally, someone paid good money for these dresses. Maybe we should ask Mr. Jamieson if he sold them." My mother looked expectantly at her sister. There was so little in their lives, even food was scarce, something like new dresses was beyond expectation. A penny for candy was a big event, until now.

Sally fingered the lace on her dress. "Yes, you may be right, but what if this really is a "milagro" or gift from God? Maybe we should think of this that way. If someone talks about missing dresses we can give them back." Fortunately for them, no one ever mentioned missing dresses and they wore them with much pride for a long time. Perhaps Aunt Sally was right after all.

My mother tossed in her sleep moaning slightly. I took a damp cloth and patted her forehead and cheeks until she became settled. How long did she have? How long could we all take this, day after day and night after night? Would her suffering become worse. Could we manage her pain? These questions burned my eyes, and my mind went to the notion of funerals and wakes, which left me sweating. I forced my thoughts to another wake, a tale Mom told me of a funeral that took place when she was a little girl. That story left us both laughing, which was a good thing.

Mom was about six or seven when one of her relatives nearby died. As was the custom, the family of the deceased placed the body in the living room and a "velatorio" or wake took place. Wakes can last for days with family members and close friends taking turns kneeling around the body praying the rosary and being somber, sometime wailing and crying. The women did this very well and with gusto; the men soon became bored and started to squirm. They would glance at each other sending silent messages with their eyes until one of them would suggest they go outside for a little drink in "memory" of the deceased. The women disapproved but kept to their vigil, sending meaningful looks that their men ignored.

In this case, soon most of the men had slipped outside to drink to the "good life" of the recently departed. One drink led to three and it was not long until the men were pretty drunk. The wake came to life then, as the men got louder and louder arguing over the fine points and not-so-fine points of the deceased. This led to pointed comments about this man or that man's personal manhood with macho comments blistering the air. When all hell broke loose the women would finally stomp out of the house, eyes blazing, rosaries dangling from their fingers. The women lit into the men, chastising them for their irreverence for the dead, deflating the machismo bubble as swiftly as a popped balloon. The men would remember their manners and why they were there, which was to pray for the dead, and by God they were going to do it!

The macho war was put on hold and the drunken men were hauled back inside where they knelt by the coffin to pray for forgiveness. Most had a tough time just staying upright as they pretended to be repentant. Another factor not in their favor was the time of year. It was August; you could fry an egg on a bald man's head, and the temperature inside the house was sweltering. The body was moving quickly into decomposition and beginning to stink. The women discreetly covered their noses with their handkerchiefs, no doubt scented with lavender water, but the men were getting sick with the combination of beer, wine, heat, and smell of decay. The body had to be moved outside to continue the wake. The men were gallant enough to close the lid and stumbled drunkenly outside, almost dropping the casket in the dirt. Once the casket was ensconced outside near a tree, the women continued mourning, urging the men folk to do the same until it was finally time to suspend the prayer vigil, at which time the women went inside to prepare the food.

Once the women were out of sight the men hightailed it around to the back to continue their own mourning ritual, drinking and talking macho. Everyone forgot the casket, lid *closed,* lying in the sun that had now angled to pour its rays directly down on the box. Mama remembers discovering the casket. At the time it scared her to death, but when she recounted it to me, we both laughed till we cried. Perhaps that is the best we could do, my mother and me—take a morbid situation and make it funny. The body had swollen so badly from the gases built up from the heat that it popped the lid of the casket open and blood and other unidentifiable body fluids were oozing out of the body, dripping down the sides of the casket onto the dirt. The stench was indescribable. No, there was no embalming back then, at least not for poor folk. Caskets were simple wooden boxes made to just fit the shape of the deceased. The women ran out praying to God and shouting, "Dios Mio!", handkerchiefs held to their faces. The men were nowhere to be seen. It would be a day that none of them would forget. When the women located them they were instructed in no uncertain terms to clean up the mess and stuff the body back into its coffin.

Repentance means different things to different people, but I think these men must have known, in their hot, hung-over conditions, that this was certainly some punishment directly from hell for their irreverence to the dead. I am sure they cleaned up more than one mess that day. My mother said that it took many days for some of them to fully recover and it was a long time before some could drink again without turning green with the memory. I am glad that the custom of the wake was gone by the time I came along. I could see my Anglo neighbors gasping at the sight of an open wooden casket in the back yard in the middle of a hot August day, women crying and praying while the men drank and sang songs to the deceased.

We took care of Mama in shifts and I spent many lonely nights sitting out in the crisp night air in a cheap, plastic lounge chair looking up at the stars. I searched for satellites that hid themselves among the stars. I stared hard, trying not to blink until I spotted one, a beautiful little speck of light that moved from the south across the sky to the north. What was it watching? Could it see me so far down here, sitting in a crummy chair while my mother died slowly inside? Could it see my face, sometimes screwed up in rage, other times crumpled with tears? I watched that speck of electronics on a journey of its own, so far above the earth, moving on a trajectory set by man to spy on the earth.

I closed my eyes when the satellite vanished from my sight, allowing my mind to wander away from here, far, far away. I went to places I had been, places that had good memories. I wished that speck of light could beam me up and away from the smell of medicine, urine, and impending death. I wished it could whisk me away from the sounds of Mom's ragged breathing and the damnable whirring of the Blue Beast. I longed to be on the beach in Cancun with all the pretty ladies and my friends drinking Negra Modelo beer and gazing out at the emerald surf, marveling at the beautiful ladies' tanned sexy legs.

How in the hell did I get here? I wondered. *How am I going to sort out my messed-up life once this illness finally ends my mother's?* Oh yes, I was painfully aware of the turmoil inside of me. After many sleepless nights, you have nothing left with which to resist your own buried skeletons and they claw their way to the surface, leaving angry, red gouges in your soul. Caring for my mother, being there during her transitional weeks, affected me. Things I did not even know I knew came up, confronting me like fractured images in a broken mirror, and the worst part of it was I could not look away, not this time.

I walked back into the house and checked on Mom. She seemed to be resting comfortably. I noticed that I was ravenous. I had not eaten anything since I'd arrived earlier for my shift, and I knew that Mom had not eaten, either, so I found something for her, we talked a little, I got her comfortable with her pillows for sleep, and then I went looking for something to eat for myself. I looked in the fridge and my mouth watered when I saw Lee's wonderful pot roast. She had told me to eat all I could because I needed some meat on my "skinny bones." Bless you, Lee, and bless your pot roast. My skinny bones would feast tonight.

<u>Dressed for church, weddings, or funerals:</u> Mama (on the right) with her sister Sally and baby brother Filbert.

<u>In the belly of the Beast:</u> From here Mama ruled the household for as long as she could. She also supervised my cooking, calling out instructions from her chair.

Chapter 5

"People will forget what you said, people will forget
what you did, but people will never forget
how you made them feel."

Maya Angelou

We did our best to settle into some kind of routine with me,
Lee, and other members of the family pitching in when they
could. For me it was like a waking dream with days and nights
running together. For Mom, it must have been a nightmare.

Looking back on it, I was aware, finally, that she never
really bitched (my term, not hers) about her plight. She
seemed more concerned about how all of us were doing. Oh
sure, she complained when the pain got so bad she could not
get comfortable in the Beast. Living and sleeping in that thing
was unimaginable to me; I wanted to take it out back, chop it
up, burn it, and watch the flames reach for the heavens—or
hell. We would, of course, return it to hospice when Mom's
ordeal came blessedly to an end. I wondered if they would
recycle it. Will some other poor, suffering soul inherit the Blue
Beast, and will he or she be able to sense the residual agony of
former occupants? Meanwhile, the gears whirred and droned
on. Sometimes I caught my mother looking at me and the pain
and terror in her eyes burned into my soul. I would have to
look away, or fiddle with the gears pretending to be useful, or
rack my brain for another tale to divert both of us.

I was thinking I should go back and recall some of our
"wonderful" times as Catholic Mexicans in Ely, Nevada,

where Dad worked in the copper mines. We found a house—
well, actually, Dad found a garage—that he converted into
living quarters. By today's standards it was a pit, but to us
it was a palace. Our former "home" was a sheepherder's
wagon, kind of like a gypsy wagon but not as romantic as
the folkloric tales. Four of us slept and pretty much lived in
that canvas-covered wagon, cooking most of what we could
outdoors, eating fish and game that we caught, sometimes
illegally. But eating was more important than gaming laws so
we danced around the law, getting caught, not getting caught,
the game of survival.

Comparitively, our new "house" was a real treat. It had no
wheels, and had one very spacious room that served as kitchen,
living room, and master bedroom. Dad even partitioned off
a tiny portion at the back of the room for Bobby and me so
we could have a little bedroom. Actually, I think it was to
give him and mom some privacy from two curious little boys.
Still, it was bitterly cold in the back cubicle (separated as it
was from the main room and the stove) and Bobby and I had
to huddle to stay warm in the winter. There was no running
water or heat and it was covered in tarpaper on the inside and
outside to act as a pathetic form of insulation.

As little boys we were not really aware, as my parents
were, of how poor we actually were. As long as we could play
we were fine, and we always managed to have hot tortillas
and beans. Bobby soon found his niche, playing marbles for
fun and profit. He was very good and I followed him around
watching him play and win. In Ely there were two forms of
working class, the Mexicans and the Indians, or, as is more
politically correct, Native Americans. Either way, we were
both the "poor folk" who did most of the cheap labor. In that
respect we had some common ground with which to relate to
each other and we played together fairly well.

I remember one little boy called Little Bear who loved
marbles. He did not have much, but he did have a nice
collection of marbles, and my brother was hell bent on winning

them. Bobby's reputation as a marble player got around pretty fast and you'd think that Little Bear would be cautious about taking him on but he seemed strangely attracted to Bobby and his fancy marbles. Although he lost again and again, he kept coming back for more. It was really sad to watch. Bobby was usually very generous and gave away marbles to other little kids, but not to Little Bear. He was almost twice Bobby's size and for some reason Bobby delighted in relieving Little Bear of his only prize possession.

There they sat, the circle drawn in the dirt, all the kids clustered around hooting and watching the mighty Little Bear and fast-fingered Bobby playing as if their lives depended on it. Like leading a sheep to slaughter, my brother aimed his trusty steely and, one by one, shot all of Little Bear's marbles out of the ring until only his prize green agate was left. *Ping!* Bobby deftly shot that last shimmering, green orb out of the ring and into his growing collection. The look of defeat on Little Bear's face got to me and I felt a twinge of guilt that my brother so ruthlessly won them like the marble hustler he was. I tried to appeal to my brother's sense of fairness.

"Bobby, why don't you give them back? They're all he has."

"No way, fair is fair and I won them. Everyone saw it. They're mine." Bobby gathered up the marbles, checking out the newest ones with interest.

"But Bobby, you always take their marbles. They know you're the best. Now they don't have anything to play with." I gave him my most imploring look.

"Nope, too bad. Maybe Little Bear and the others should learn to play better." Bobby just shrugged. My brother was a marble junkie; he was obsessed with marbles. I guess he couldn't help himself. And it was something that gave him some notoriety—a reputation. His stash of shiny marbles was a visible indicator of his success among our poor community of raggedy kids and I could not hold that against him.

It was on the same day that Little Bear "lost all his marbles" that we had our first real scare while living at the mines. Just as Bobby was putting away his winnings and the kids were trying to talk him into another match, we heard the terrible keening wail of the town siren. It made my flesh crawl and my hair stood on end with a sense of terrible foreboding. Sirens did not go off to celebrate good tidings, at least not in Ely. Bobby and I looked at each other knowing that Dad and Uncle Joey worked in the mines. We grabbed our stuff, stuffing Bobby's marbles into the little cloth bag Mama made for him, and raced home. As soon as we arrived, Aunt Alma drove up, skidding to a stop in her old Ford pickup, sending a cloud of dust into the air.

"Stella, Stella!" she screamed. "We gotta go right now! There's been an accident at the mine!"

Mom raced out of the house, shouting, "You boys get in the truck, quick now!"

Aunt Alma ground the gears getting the old truck into action and we bounced off toward the mine.

"Alma, do you think C and Joey are okay? I know God will take care of them but. . ." My mother's voice trailed off and she sat silently in the back of the truck with her arms wound tightly around Bobby and me.

I whispered to Bobby, "Do you think Daddy is okay?" Bobby's face was pale but he whispered back, "Sure. Daddy is tough. Nothin' can hurt him, or Uncle Joey either."

At the mine, trucks and ambulances were running in and out of the area and people were clustered all about, some of them crying, some looking shell-shocked, some just silently praying. The siren was still screaming, making things worse. I felt my insides turn to jelly.

"Please don't let Daddy be hurt, please!" I prayed in my most fervent voice. I started to cry and Bobby turned on me.

"Oh, don't be such a baby. Dad's tough; I just told you so." Mama and Aunt Alma ran around tugging on the sleeves of miners who were milling about, asking about my dad and Uncle Joey.

"Have you seen my husband? Have you seen Celio Benavidez? What about Joe Benavidez, is he okay?" My mother began to panic and her voice became shrill. "Does anyone know ANYTHING?!!"

Finally, a tall miner with a blackened face and carrying his carbide lantern in his hand worked his way through the crowd to my mother and aunt. It was Lefty, my Dad's best friend. He grabbed my mother by the arm. "Stella, Alma, it's okay. Joe is down there as part of the rescue team, helping the guys who are hurt get out, and C is running the cage. They're both okay and not hurt. But they're gonna be busy for a while. You need to go home and wait." My mother nearly fainted with relief.

Others weren't so lucky. It took three days to get all the miners out and five of them did not make it out alive. We did not see Dad for three days when the rescue was complete. He shuffled into the house exhausted and filthy, the ordeal of what he had experienced visible on his face streaked with grime. Mama ran up to him, threw her arms around his neck and cried, "Oh, C, I was so worried. I would die without you."

He hugged her and held her out at arm's length looking at her. "Stella, you know I can take care of myself. Now where are the boys?"

Pulling herself together, with a little sniffle, she replied, "Oh, they're probably outside somewhere playing marbles with the other boys. How about some hot chili and beans?"

Mama stirred and moaned a bit. I went over to her and touched her hand. She turned to me and tried to smile. "Ah, hijo, you are still here. I was dreaming. Can you adjust this pillow a little, please?"

I smiled back at her, held up two fingers, and asked, "How many fingers, Mom?"

She sighed. For me she played the game, one more time, maybe two. "Why, three fingers, Danny, I see three. Now what have you been doing while I was sleeping?"

I looked at her a little sheepishly. "I was really thinking about the time when we lived in Ely, about Bobby and his marbles and Daddy and Uncle Joey and the mine collapse."

"Oh, yes, that was quite a scare." My mother looked like she was thinking of something else.

"What is it, Mom? What are you thinking?" Mom shifted her body a little, grimaced at a small twinge, and replied, "The story I was remembering is not a good one, son. And I remember that this story always made you angry and I can't say I liked it much myself when I heard it. But I think it helped me understand your father a little better. Ely was not a very good place for Mexicans and it was not good for the Indians living there, either."

Dad, Bobby, and I had just stepped out of the little store in downtown Ely and were nose-deep into our double-dip ice cream cones. It was payday and we could always count on ice cream and a whole quarter to go to the movies. For us, payday was like a carnival day and life was good—except on this day. On this day, life provided a reality check.

"Hey, you Mexicans, get the hell off the sidewalk. Go walk in the street where you belong!" The nasty shout came from a tall, skinny young man behind us. Dad wheeled around on the man who was twice our size but smaller than Dad.

"What did you say?" Dad's voice was low and hard.

"Ya heard me. What the hell are you Mexicans doin' on our sidewalk?" The man stood in front of Dad like he owned the town, with his head cocked to one side.

Dad balled his hands into fists. "Why, you silly son of a bitch. I'd kick your ass, but I'm too big and too old for you!"

The man smirked. "Don't worry, greaser. You couldn't get to me anyway. You'd fall on your ass from all that *grease* first."

Dad stepped back and slowly studied the man from top to bottom. "Well, now that I look at you, I won't kick your ass—my boys here will do it."

The man's crooked smile grew wider. "Me against two little snot-nosed greasers? Yeah, sure."

Dad looked down at Bobby and me, huddled by his legs, and said the unthinkable: "Now, Bobby, I want you to get him around the neck and Danny, you get him around the legs. And remember: Every time he hits you and you don't hit him back, I'm gonna swat you with my belt. Now go get him!"

Oh shit. I looked at Bobby. This guy, though a young man, was at least five hundred feet tall and weighed a thousand pounds, at least in the eyes of one little boy.

"Bobby, you go first, okay?"

Bobby snarled at me, "You little chicken shit! We both go and do what Daddy says."

I gulped. "Okay, but I'm scared!"

Bobby grabbed my arm and shoved me. "Ah, Danny, you're always scared. Now go!"

With my heart in my throat I threw myself at the man, wrapping my arms around his legs and holding on with all I had, just as Dad told me to. Bobby catapulted himself off the ground up onto the guy's body, crawling and punching his way to the top. At first the guy was so stunned he just stood there with a look of shock on his face. Finally he began kicking at me with his free leg, trying to dislodge me while pushing on Bobby's head to keep him from scratching his neck. It must have been quite a sight. For me, it was fear turned to hate and then survival and I hung on. Finally, the man got fed up with these two nasty mosquitoes driving him nuts and called out, "Okay, okay, I quit! It's not worth it. Call off your dogs."

Dad stood his ground. "Not until you apologize and never call us greasers or dirty Mexicans again, ya hear?"

"Ah fuck it! Okay, I apologize, I won't do it again, at least not to you and your kids. Now call 'em off!" We slid off the man's body and, trembling, went back to our father, awaiting further instructions and perhaps some explanation of what just happened. Bobby seemed pumped up by it; I was really confused and amazed that I did not pee my pants.

Dad knelt down to eye level with us. "You boys did real good. You did not back down and showed you weren't afraid to fight for yourselves. I want you to remember something here. Don't ever, ever let anyone call you a Mexican. We ain't no damn Mexicans. We're Spanish. You got that? We're Spanish."

My little mind turned in on itself. Huh? We're not Spanish; nobody told me we were Spanish. We're from Mexico. What was Dad thinking? Later I learned a lot about my father's shame and his humiliation about his Mexican heritage. And some of that lived on in me.

Dad patted our heads and we headed home. As we looked up at him, he smiled. "And one more thing: Don't tell your mother about this. It's just between us men, okay?"

Yeah, sure. Mama was the All-Knowing One and had a direct connection with God. We knew she would find out somehow, some way.

<u>Celio Benavidez:</u> Dad was an excellent shot and could bring home the bacon—or elk—with ease. Having a little sip of something later to celebrate good hunting didn't hurt, either.

<u>Ely, Nevada:</u> Bobby and me (on the left) outside our tar paper, one-room shack. Note the rakish tilt of my hat. My brother was definitely the Marble King of Ely.

Chapter 6

"Power is the strength and the ability to see yourself through your own eyes and not through the eyes of another."

Agnes Whistling Elk

As I walked into the house to begin my shift, I ran into my sister. "How did Mom do today, Lee?" I watched her face for any sign of something that would indicate a turn for the worse.

"She had a pretty good day, Dan. The pain seemed to be under control." I sighed inwardly with relief. Hopefully my shift would be easy this time. There was also the mouthwatering aroma of one of Lee's famous pot roasts coming from the kitchen.

Lee looked me up and down. "Be sure to eat some of that pot roast, Dan. You look too skinny."

I assured her I would. Actually, I thought about diving face first into that steaming pot, but first I needed to check on Mom. I walked in and found her just waking up from her snooze.

"Hi, Mom, how are you today? Are you hungry?" I gave her a little hug. It may have been my imagination or the lighting but Mom seemed a little brighter and her color did not look quite so sallow.

"Hi, son. I am doing okay. Maybe I could eat just a little something."

I fixed us a couple of plates and went in to encourage Mom through the long process of getting food into her. That usually meant distracting her with something on the one hand while

I kept food going into her with the other. She knew it, too, because she said, "Tell me one of our stories while I eat, hijo."

"Which one, Mama?" I asked between bites.

"Oh, how about the one where you boys went with your dad to Los Angeles?"

After being discharged from the army, my Uncle Lee moved to Los Angeles. While there, he got the notion that he and my dad could make a good living by going into the roofing business together. My mom was a little reluctant, but Dad, ready for a change, was eager to give it a go. It was arranged that Mom would go with Uncle Lee in his '36 Ford and we would follow shortly after in the old pickup.

Mom grabbed Dad in a hug as they said their goodbyes. "Now, C, you be careful. Don't let the boys ride in the back of the truck cause it's not safe and it's hot and take plenty of water, and…"

Dad held Mom out at arm's length and laughed. "Stella, you worry too much. This is a good move and I am getting out of those damn mines that are nothing but underground living graveyards. And we both hate it here." Then Mama and Uncle Lee headed off down the road and we waved until we could not see the truck anymore.

Dad finished the last minute loading and tying down the stuff on our 1934 Dodge pickup. Then we said our final goodbyes to our friends and Uncle Sam and his wife Sonia who were keeping our beloved cocker spaniel, Goldy, because we couldn't take her along. There were lots of hugs, slaps on the back, and a few tears as we all pretended to be brave about leaving. We promised to try to come back the next spring to visit or maybe they could come see us but we knew that was probably unlikely.

Uncle Sam slapped my dad on the back. "You sure that old rust bucket you call a truck's gonna even make it to California? It's older than hell and it overheats. You sure you got plenty of water, C?"

My dad hugged Uncle Sam. "You sound like my wife, Sam. We'll be fine. I got it all figured out and we got what we need. Don't you worry. You take care of you, okay?"

Our old Dodge looked quite the sight piled high with all our meager possessions and we wondered if it would even move under all that weight. Bobby and I crammed ourselves into the front seat with Dad and we were off, not exactly moving fast, but we were moving, the engine wheezing under the load and the heat. We were excited and a little sad at the same time. We were leaving a place where, for the most part, the Mexicans were hated almost more than the Native Americans, and God knows Dad had more than one close call with mine catastrophes. On the other hand, we did make some friends; misery brings people together and even Bobby's old nemesis, Little Bear, was sad to see us go. I imagined him looking forward to taking back his title of undisputed marble king.

After a while on the road Bobby piped up. "Daddy, I'm thirsty."

Dad looked up the road for a place to pull over. "Okay, boys, we'll stop up there by a wide spot on the side of the road. We need to stop anyway 'cause I think the truck might be overheating and I need to add some water to the radiator." Just as we pulled over and Dad turned off the engine, a huge plume of white steam hissed out from under the hood. Dad got a serious look on his face. "Hmmm, it's hotter than I thought. We're gonna have to wait a few minutes for it to cool down; I'll get the water can from the back."

Bobby and I waited anxiously for Dad to get the water. We were sweating so much our shirts stuck to our bodies and the water was dripping off our noses. Crowded into the front seat we felt like we were going to melt.   Dad came back and poured water into a couple of cups and we practically inhaled it we were so thirsty. But no sooner had the water gone down we knew something was very wrong. Bobby and I starting spitting and gagging, trying to get the taste out of our mouths.

"Daddy, the water tastes funny."

Dad took the cup, tasted the water, and immediately spit it out, swearing. "Damn that Joey. He told me this can was clean, but it had gasoline in it. Don't drink it, boys. You'll get sick."

"But Daddy, we're real thirsty," I whined.

Dad's face turned grim. "Sorry, but there's nothin' I can do about it now. We have to wait until we get to a gas station." We were almost in tears but we knew better than to press the point. We had no idea how far the next gas station would be, we were all hot and thirsty, and Dad's mood was turning foul. We had to sweat it out, literally, at least whatever stinky sweat we had left.

Five thirsty hours later Bobby spotted the gas station first. "Look, Daddy, there's a gas station!" It was the most beautiful thing we had ever seen, like an oasis to three parched travelers. As the truck came to a wheezing stop, the attendant showed up at Dad's side of the truck.

"Can I help you, sir?" Dad gave him a big smile. "You sure can. You can fill 'er up, check the oil and tires, and oh yeah, where is the water?"

The attendant looked at Dad a moment and replied, "How much water you want? It's a dollar a gallon."

Dad nearly choked. "A dollar a gallon! I never heard of anybody selling water. Why, it should be free!"

The attendant crossed his arms and took a hard stance. "Well, you heard about it now, and if you don't like it you can just go somewhere else where maybe they'll give you some for free, if you want to wait that long."

Dad's face and neck were turning red, maybe from the heat and maybe from a slow, simmering anger. "But me and my boys are real thirsty. We haven't had anything to drink since we left Ely 'cause the water we have is bad."

The attendant got a real strange look on his face. It was not a nice look and it made me really nervous.

"Daddy, the cokes are only a nickel, can't we have a Coke, please?"

Dad turned then and looked at Bobby and me. "Sure, boys, here's fifty cents. Go buy ten of them. I'll be damned if I'll pay a dollar a gallon for something that should be free to anyone. Besides, we only have five dollars and we have to make it last."

We bought the Cokes and the gas and got back on the road. We didn't say much for a while. At last I voiced what we probably were all thinking. "You know, Daddy, I think that man did not want us to have the water because he thinks we're just dumb Mexicans." Dad looked at me with an expression that caused me to go very quiet while Bobby dropped his eyes and stared at something on the floor. No one said another word for many, many miles.

In her chair Mom was quiet for a bit. "You know, son, we get many lessons in life. They can either make us bitter or they can make us strong. I still get a little sad when I hear stories like that. It is not fair to little boys who are so young to have to learn of such things."

I took one of Mom's hands. "You know, Ma, we learned a lot of tough lessons and some of them still make me mad, but mostly, I think we came out pretty good and we learned how to handle ourselves around the gringos. I will tell you a story that I think is kind of funny, but Bobby and me were a little dishonest with some of the stuff we did. I am just glad you did not find out about it at the time because you would have stopped us and we were so proud of the money we brought home. Promise you won't get mad, okay? It was a long time ago."

Mom gave me that piercing "Now what are you going to tell me?" look and settled back into the chair, her hands folded in her lap.

We were living in Compton, California, at the time and Bobby had just turned nine. We'd been selling newspapers on street corners for over a year, starting when Bobby was eight and I was six. We took all the money we earned home to Mom for the household expenses and at the end of the month she would give each of us $5.00. Flush with cash we would head to Long Beach on the streetcar and ride the roller coaster over and over. Our record was twenty-five rides in a row. In between we stuffed ourselves with hot dogs and cotton candy. We felt so grown up, two little boys, ages nine and seven, with money to spend all by ourselves doing whatever we wanted for the day.

We peddled papers for the Los Angeles Herald Express, who stacked the papers ten bundles high with fifty papers per bundle. They were left on the curb at the intersection of East Vernon Ave. and South Alameda Street.

"Bobby, what corner do you want?" I asked my brother.

Bobby pointed. "I'll take the corner across the street this time."

I always disagreed. "How come you always get the good corners? After all, I'm the boss, right?"

"Yeah, you're the boss, but I'm still older and smarter. Besides, I think it's time we switch corners." Bobby wandered off across the intersection carrying two bundles with him.

I stepped out between the lanes of busy traffic on Alameda, cars and trucks zipping by inches from my elbows and began working the street. "Express here! Get your paper Express here!" The cars would stop, an arm would shove a nickel out the window and I would hand them a paper.

One day I watched a big Cummings diesel truck rumble up next to me and stop. I cringed a bit because the truck and driver looked so big and ominous. The driver leaned out the window laughing as I tried to carefully hand him his paper. He yelled above the roar of the engine, "Here it comes, boy! Hang on to your hat! This will make your toes curl!" Then he would press the nickel into my hand. The static electricity from the charged-up truck would give me what felt like a jolt from hell. The driver thought it was hilarious. "How was that, boy? A little weak this time, was it? I'll save a bigger jolt for you next time." Then he would roar off. Needless to say, I hated truck drivers. It was a favorite trick they played on L.A. paper boys. The streetcar was another good place to sell papers. I would anticipate some good sales as it pulled up, packed with people, the long connecting rod with its little wheel at the end sparking when it came in contact with the charged power line above it. Halting at the intersection, people would hang out the windows yelling, "Hey, boy, paper here. Hey, boy, over here, over here."

I worked the streetcars front to back. On this particular day a grisly faced man with big bushy eyebrows and a permanent frown on his face yelled louder than anyone else. "Hey you, you little Mex! Over here, dammit! Bring me a paper, quick, before the damned car leaves. You hear me, boy?"

Ah, yes, I loved this kind of guy, and he was about to make my day. I hurried over to his window. He handed me a dollar bill. "Hurry up, you little Mex! Give me my damn change before this car pulls out!" Now I actually had an apron full of change, but I pretended to fumble around trying to find the correct amount, stalling until the light changed. He kept yelling, I kept stalling, until finally the conductor clanged the bell and the streetcar pulled out. By this time the guy was practically spitting at me. "Damn you, you give me my change!" I would look up innocently, still fumbling, and yell, "Sorry, sir, I'll be sure to get you tomorrow!" The car would pull off with the guy still hollering out the window. Wahoo! Another coup for the Mexican boy. Bobby and me made mucho bucks this way. We just loved the mean gringos in business suits with dollar bills.

We changed corners every week, switching roles so we did not meet the same gringos who might recognize us (although all Mexicans probably look alike to them). Mom and Dad were amazed at the amount of money we made, and we did not enlighten them about our less-than-honest methods. I know Dad would have taken his razor strap to our little butts if he knew. Mom would have probably done a lot of loud praying for our immortal souls as well as cut us off from our roller coaster days. But we were basically snot-nosed kids learning the ropes on the streets of Compton. And we learned fast.

Our neighborhood in Compton was pretty much all black except for the Mexicans. Since we were also dark-skinned we did not concern ourselves with the lack of whiteness on Staunton Ave. We all got along in the way street kids did, scrapping amongst ourselves, mainly over who got the best street corners. Bobby and I developed our reputations early on as two tough kids who held onto their territory, and we did not hesitate to defend it. Many was the night we walked home in the polluted Los Angeles evening air, bloodied and bruised from defending our turf. We never lost. We were mean little bastards and Bobby could and would kick anyone's ass. All the other little hoodlums were scared of him. That was one of the few advantages of having a bossy older brother on the streets of L.A.

You had to be tough in the 'hood if you wanted to survive. At the Vernon City inner-city school where we went, there were some really bad dudes who spent their days at the school and their nights at a nearby reform facility. The teachers could barely control the chaos that reigned there. And you did not dare back away from any scrap that came your way or you were destined to become everyone's whipping boy. You even had to have backup when you went to the bathroom or you might not come out in one piece.

The only thing I learned there was how not to get caught doing things you weren't supposed to do. If you did get caught, the teachers used a sawed-off boat paddle that rendered your backside so bruised you could not sit for a week. So between the teachers' paddles and the regular bad asses from the reform school, you had to learn survival techniques. For me learning my *abc*'s meant "always be careful."

In looking back at all that, I really pity our poor mother. I am sure she must have thought we were going straight to hell. We were getting way out of hand. So she did the only thing a good Catholic mother could do. We were transferred to Holy Cross Catholic School.

It was a rough transition at first. We were conditioned to beat the crap out of anyone who even looked at us cross-eyed. We were not used to smiles that were actually smiles of welcome. For the first few weeks, the Carmelite nuns and the Jesuit priests had their hands full with the little Mexican brothers from the 'hood. For us it was easier to take the kid out of the 'hood than it was to take the 'hood out of the kid. Fortunately, or unfortunately depending on your point of view, Father Gregory had his own customized boat paddle and in a very short time the only things Bobby and I feared were not the meek and mild white kids from rich families but the meetings with Father Gregory and his boat paddle.

Before we moved to New Mexico, we had been transformed into good little Catholics. I was even, much to Mama's joy, an altar boy at the 8 a.m. mass on Sundays. I actually believed if I accidentally touched the sacred chalice while I was pouring wine for the good padre I would burn in Hell. Even to this day, as old as I am, I still get a quick, uneasy feeling when I scarf down a meaty, greasy hamburger on Fridays, wondering for just a second how many Hail Mary's I would have to say to work off this venial sin.

Thinking we would be moving on to something better, Dad moved us to Los Duranes, one of the barrios of Albuquerque, New Mexico. There he and my Uncle Elias opened up a small service station in Los Barelas, one of the toughest barrios there. For Bobby and me it was like jumping from the frying pan into a roasting pit. Our four-room adobe house had no running water or gas. It was located on a dirt road that ran next to the cornfields and half a mile from the Rio Grande River. The outhouse was out back and a hundred feet from it was the well from which we hand-pumped water for the family needs. We took a bath in the big washtub once a week right after Mom finished the laundry. We hated bath and laundry day because Bobby and I had to haul all that water into the

house. I remember whining a lot about it. Now I wonder just
how my mother managed. Her work started when she got up
at the crack of dawn and did not end until she collapsed in bed
at night. How amazing it must have been when she got her
very first indoor bathroom or major appliance.

Our little house had one main room (about 150 square
feet) that functioned as a combination bedroom for Bobby
and me, a washroom to do the clothes, and a kitchen. Our
grandmother also lived with us. Since she was too old to go
to the outhouse at night, I had the dubious honor of emptying
her chamber pot every morning before I left for school. Bobby
was not willing to bargain for anything to exchange that chore.
He got so tired of me complaining about it that he threatened
to stuff a quart of beans down my throat so I'd blow farts for a
month. Grandma slept in what was officially called our living
room while Mom, Dad, and my two baby sisters occupied the
two tiny bedrooms.

Mom put Bobby and me into Sacred Heart School in the
middle of the Barelas barrio. Word got out that we were "bad
ass" boys from L.A., so we got tested early on. When one of
the meanest bullies, Lencho, started harassing us, Bobby said
to me, "Okay, Danny, I gotta kick Lencho's ass." I tried to tell
Bobby that he was too big and mean and he had the rest of the
school bullies behind him. But Bobby knew the score and told
me that he had to do it or we wouldn't have any peace there
and would be picked on forever.

Bobby picked his time after class one day when Lencho
was walking by with his amigos. Bobby stepped out in front
of Lencho and said, "Hey, Lencho, you look like a girl with
that funny shirt you have on."

Lencho, of course, stopped dead in his tracks. "What did
you say to me? I'm gonna kick your ass!"

Bobby did not say anything else. He moved fast as
lightening and laid a haymaker right hook on Lencho's jaw.
As he was toppling to the ground, Bobby stayed on him
pummeling and kicking him. As Lencho lay there moaning

in pain, Bobby turned to the other bullies and simply asked, "Who's next?" We were never messed with again.

Through high school, I worked at a store called Payless Grocery right in the heart of the Barelas Barrio. I bagged and delivered groceries, cleaned floors, and scraped meat blocks. Eventually, with help from the owners, I was trained to be a card-carrying journeyman meat-cutter or butcher. That got me a job at a Kroger store in a fancier part of Albuquerque. The manager was hesitant to hire me because he knew I was of an age that qualified me for the draft, and on top of that I had a Selective Service 1-A classification. He was concerned that he would put the training time in and I would get drafted. But my meat-cutting qualifications won out and he hired me anyway.

Wow! How good was this, a great job in a nice part of town? I was on the first rung of the ladder of my climb out of the barrio. I had a little twinge that the manager might be right, but then again he could be wrong. I could go down and just sign up for the army and get it over with, but I could also be making good money at this new job and establish myself in this position as one of Kroger's butchers. Nah, I'd take my chances. Maybe my number would be somewhere way at the bottom of the heap.

Yeah right. Nine months later I was in the army. So much for my new career as "Dan the Meat Man."

Chapter 7

"The greatest hazard of all, losing one's self, can occur very
quietly in the world, as if it were nothing at all."

Soren Kierkegaard

Mom was at war with her disease and losing ground,
succumbing to a DMZ (demilitarized zone) within that simply
afforded her a moment of comfort here and there relatively
devoid of pain. In those last months, we all retreated to our
individual escape zones in our minds, just getting by hour
after hour on our respective shifts, plastic smiles on our faces
as we passed each other commenting, "She had a good night."
On many of my shifts I dozed off and was catapulted back to
memories I thought I had long trained myself to forget. But
extreme exhaustion breaks down even the best defenses, and I
found myself back in the war zone.

I was doing great at Kroger's as a meat cutter. I had myself
a new car, money in my pocket . . . and the threat of the draft
hanging over me. Finally I got fed up being anxious waiting for
the notice and decided to get it over with. I marched down to
the selective service office and said, "Take me." It was done.

How ironic, where once I was a butcher cutting, inspecting
and selling meat, I was now going to be a "piece of meat"
waiting to be inspected by the U.S. Government. About
two weeks after I signed the papers, I found myself lined up
naked with about twenty other draftees, our hands pressed up
against the wall. Nobody said much; some tried to make snide
remarks, but they sounded pretty pitiful. We were told to stand

there and shut up. The army doc walked in and shouted at us, "Keep leaning against the wall and raise your right foot." He checked our right feet followed by our left feet, and then yelled, "Okay, bend over and spread your cheeks." Then he shouted out various observations to some invisible aide till he got to the end of the line. One guy piped up that he had bad stomach problems, had had them all his life, and had difficulty keeping food down. The doc just snorted and said something to the effect of, "No problem, you'll make a good cook, with plenty to eat after you barf." The draftee whined, "But I'm not fit to serve!" The doc replied that he heard him, made a note, and reminded him he would still make a good cook. Case closed. And with that I was a fully inspected Grade A piece of meat, property of the U.S. Army.

It was a windy, dreary day when I flew out of the Albuquerque airport for the Army. Mom and my little sister took me to the airport and I remember Mom crying and my sister hugging me too hard. I was trying to be macho about the whole thing, telling Mom it was no big deal and I would be back before she knew it. But then Mom said, "God take care of you." That finished me and I broke out sobbing.

I had never really been away from home and I was scared out of my mind. I swiped at the tears with the back of my hand, plastered a stupid smile on my face, waved goodbye, and boarded the plane to Los Angeles.

From Los Angeles I boarded the train to Ft. Ord for basic training. As soon as we were on our way I headed, of course, to the bar car, where I met two other Latino dudes from L.A. who were also on their way to Ft. Ord. In no time at all we were doing some heavy duty beer drinking commiserating on our fates. I guess I got pretty shit-faced because what happened next was a bit surreal. Back then I did not know what mentally challenged was about or some types of special needs that might have hampered the dude's ability to communicate properly, but I do know I must have put my foot in it. We were getting funny and jibing each other a bit when I must have ramped up the harassing and crossed the line. I noticed that one of the guys didn't talk much but had this perpetual grin on his face that didn't change. He just kept smiling at me and nodding occasionally. Finally, like an ass, I turned to him and asked, "Yo, vato, what the hell is wrong with you? You some kind of dummy? Can't you talk?"

Quicker than snot his buddy slammed down his beer and rounded on me. "Hey man, fuck off! Leave him alone!"

Taken aback I threw up my hands and got defensive. "Hey, go fuck yourself. I was just joking." In a flash he grabbed me by the collar and laid a massive punch to my eye and a jab to my nose. My head hit the table and I was down for the count. My two new Latino "buddies" took off.

I was pretty much ignored until a good-hearted conductor saw me hunched over the table with a bloody nose and an eye that was rapidly changing color and swelling shut. He took one look and exclaimed, "Oh my God, what happened to you! Christ, here's a napkin for your nose and I'll be right back with something for your eye. It looks real bad!" He returned shortly with a big ol' steak that he put over my eye. On a better day I would have loved that steak medium rare with some potatoes on the side.

Until our arrival the next morning, I spent the time lying in my bunk with the steak aging on my eye which was now swollen black and blue. At Ft. Ord the captain inspected the new draftees as we lined up at attention. Once he saw me with my battered face he got this glint in his eye and got right in front of me. Uh-oh. As I stood at attention, he shouted (or rather spit) in my face, "Soldier, what the hell happened to you? Jesus, you look like shit! You don't look like an American soldier. You look like a friggin bum!" My knees were knocking but I did not dare move. He wasn't done. "Don't you even think about going off base looking like that, do you hear me, soldier?"

I responded in what I thought was appropriately loud and respectful, "Yes, I hear you." He took a step back and looked shocked. Then he shouted even louder, "What the hell is that? You're talking to an officer. It's 'Yes, sir!' to you and don't you ever forget it!" My mouth was so dry I could barely get out, "Yes, sir! Sir!" And so began my first experience in the Army.

After a couple of weeks at good old Ft. Ord, my head was shaved, my civilian clothes in moth balls, and my brain thoroughly washed of everything but "Yes, sir, no, sir" and "Yes, Sergeant, no, Sergeant." In my new uniform I was packed off to Ft. Carson, Colorado, for basic training. Why I went through Ft. Ord before Ft. Carson is still baffling to me, but was probably some typical army SNAFU (situation normal, all fucked up) about where I was really supposed to be for basic. My job was to keep my mouth shut, follow orders, and, of course, become all that I could be in the Army.

Violence, wherever it is or whatever its form, plays on the rational mind. Are you for it or against it? Are you crazy for thinking it is crazy? Are there acceptable forms? Are we programmed to accept it depending on just how much violence, based on what our leaders tell us, it takes to maintain peace? That is an oxymoronic statement in my not-so-humble view.

No one tells a young man barely out of his teens that the remainder of his youth will be ripped away in a few short weeks or months, with no mama to offer up cookies and milk or hot tortillas and chili. Imagine the sound of gunfire, or that special zinging sound of shrapnel from an explosion of fragmentation grenades as they fly through the air right past your head, or the distinct short bursts of machine gun fire, burning themselves indelibly on your memory. No Fourth of July can ever top that.

For me there was also the ill-fated decision to zonk out right next to a tank at night, thinking it a safe place to be, only to be tossed into the air when it began blasting away before dawn. That will certainly have you crapping in your fatigues.

And then there was the time we were sitting in the dirt, waiting for help after our deuce and a half went crashing out

of control and careened down an embankment landing upside-
down. Amazingly we suffered nothing more serious than a
few bumps and bruises. There we sat, two black guys and one
brown trying to be macho, laughing and being smart-asses to
cover up the fact that we almost bought the farm and were
seriously shaken up about being in the wrong place at the
wrong time for the wrong reason. I guess it's things like that
that make men out of boys, but it also raises the question,
what IS the right place at the right time for the right reason? I
don't recall ever getting to vote on that.

I was a very green new recruit and Platoon Sergeant
Wilson was inches from my face as we stood in formation.

"Soldier, are you eyeballing me?"

I replied loudly but hopefully correctly this time, "No,
Sergeant, I am not!"

"Bullshit!" he spat back. "You are too eyeballing me, so
cut it out or I'll poke your eyes out and skull fuck you!"

I turned my eyes to the side trying not to sweat. "Yes, sir.
I understand, sir."

He got closer. "Sir?! I ain't no fuckin', sir. Drop down and
give me twenty, you sorry piece of shit-for-brains soldier!" At
the time I was young and scared and it all seemed like serious
shit, now the absurdity of it makes me laugh.

While serving in the Army we often spent weeks out in
the field living in pup tents, sleeping in our fart sacks, and
eating c–rations. Obviously we got really filthy, so on a daily
basis, after rousting ourselves in the morning, we indulged in
what we called "whore baths" using our helmets as basins. We
bathed what body parts we could reach shedding the bigger
chunks of dirt and/or critters that may have taken up residence
on our bodies. Once in a while, when we were out in the field
longer than usual, we would be taken to an Air Force base for
some R & R, real showers, and mess hall food, not c-rations.
The Air Force types shuddered when they saw us coming
and for good reason. Piling out of our army trucks, we were
raunchy, loud, hungry, testy GI's looking for fun or trouble,

whichever came first. The officers and sergeants should have made some small effort to keep us in line, but they needed a break as much as we did, so they turned their heads the other way whenever possible.

We terrorized the place from the moment we set foot there. The flyboys certainly hated to see us come and they were on orders to share their base with us periodically. We thought the flyboys were arrogant wusses who really did not know what serving your country was all about. Hindsight truly can be 20/20; we really were jerks, but at the time we thought we were "da bomb" and no one could stop us having our fun. We dirtied their showers, flipped off the airmen on base because we thought they looked down their noses at us, and when we were in the PX we ripped off anything we could stuff into our fatigue pockets. When the flyboys gave us crusty looks or came forward as if to accuse us, we would take the offensive by being low and dirty. "Don't even try to fuck with us, you hear? Back off! Don't even go there!" And they would back off, and sort of look the other way like they didn't see anything going on. Yeah, absolutely embarrassing to think about now. We acted like thugs, but our sense of reality back then was what it was, just dirty out-of-control GI's coming back into civilization from weeks in the rain and mud, experiencing our own kind of re-entry. It wasn't pretty to those who "welcomed" us.

The Air Force, in its infinite wisdom, anticipated what we were capable of and did what it could to accommodate us as well as maintain damage control to some degree. A makeshift "beer hall" was put up for us set well away from the main base and facilities. It was there the grungy Army boys could, without the red tape of protocol, raise hell and get shit-faced, not necessarily in that order. Of course the tent had no amenities such as indoor plumbing, so they dug a large dirt "poop pit," really nothing more than a large hole in the ground with a couple of large planks placed across the thing so you could squat and take a crap. This outdoor latrine with no doors was about twenty yards from the "beer hall" and seemed to do the job for boozed-up

GI's who had overstuffed themselves with mess hall food. But then relief was relief no matter how you spelled it.

One evening, all squeaky clean from showering and messing up the flyboys' shower facilities, we were ready to do some serious drinking and getting down, so away we went to the "beer hall." We went at it with gusto, guzzling large quantities of beer and staggering out every now and then to tend to the call of nature. Eventually, the beer ran out and my buddies Shuraba, Dave, Al, Silas, and I (totally drunk by this time) left for the billets to sleep off the night's festivities. After a few yards into the black night, we noticed Silas was missing. We started looking but couldn't find him until we heard this pathetic drunken cry, "Hey youse guys! Help me! Help me!" We followed his cries and found him sprawled in the poop pit covered in, well, you guessed it—everything. We started laughing our heads off, holding our noses while he moaned and pleaded till we finally hoisted his steaming, stinking ass out of there. Crazy, huh? Yet it all made sense then, at least in the moment.

On other occasions, if we were lucky, we were given special passes to go to the local village and hang out, drinking beer and eating wiener schnitzel at one of the gasthauses. I was not a very tall or very big man but I was sure a scrappy little s.o.b. I came from a long line of scrappy survivalists; just ask my brother. Because of my youthful looks, my badass buddies—and others who wore Green Beret-type caps on their heads—liked to use me to help them mess with the flyboys. They would invite me over, buy me some beers all buddy-like, and then lay out a plan. Once I was pretty juiced, I would go over and bad-mouth a table of flyboys until they got good and pissed off. I would say things like, "Hey, you flyboy, you look funny as shit in your bus driver suit. What a bunch of candy-ass bus drivers you are." When they got angry enough to stand up and chase me, I would run back toward my badass buds, who would charge into the fray and get a good brawl going. I usually ducked under a table and worked my way to the exit. Usually only the berets were left, and we all staggered out together, clapping each other on the backs and laughing over our victory.

Looking back on it, we always started the fights not the airmen. Hmmm. And we thought THEY were the idiots. We thought they did not understand us and I know we had no clue who they were and what they stood for. Yeah, I know, all wrong reasons, but that was then. Thinking back on it, they were the wiser of the two factions.

I cannot let my Army career fade into the dust without addressing some of the hoopla around the "Don't ask, don't tell" policy concerning gays in the service. Give me a break. Don't even go there unless you were there in the trenches. It was not like we went around broadcasting who was straight and who was gay, but most of us knew who was who and we let it go. We were soldiers and depended on each other for our wellbeing. We did not really give a damn and the bottom line was we belonged to the same fraternity of soldiers where color, religion, and sexual persuasion took a back seat to more pressing matters of the moment. Which in fact brings me to a rather harmless and humorous story that involved me personally, and still makes me laugh when I think about it.

After one of our R & R's, we all got drunk, as was usually the case, and some trucks were sent to haul us back to our campsite. Because we were so sloshed many of us were literally tossed into the backs of the trucks. I am sure many of us remember little about that evening, but a few did, especially me. When we were tossed into the truck, some laughing and some almost unconscious, I realized that I was pretty much on the bottom of the heap. On top of me, nose-to-nose, was Sgt. B., our platoon sergeant who was totally sloshed. As we went down the bumpy road, I could feel his mustache nuzzling my ear, and I sobered up really fast when I realized he was trying to kiss me. I yelled at the top of my lungs, "No, Sergeant, no! Stop it! It's me, Dan!" Some of the guys close to me were coherent enough to hear that exchange and the next morning as I crossed the campsite perimeter to get some strong coffee, some of my buddies shouted, "Dan, where's your boyfriend?" And then they made loud lip-smacking sounds and blew kisses at me. I stood there looking at the bunch of them with a shit-eating grin on my face and flipped them the bird. Everyone burst out laughing and hooting, having one hell of a good time poking fun at me, and then it was over. After that it was business as usual, no big friggin deal. It was never mentioned again, certainly not by Sergeant B. or me, and in due time we were once again back to being just GI's doing what we did best, which was watching out for each other's back.

And yet, with all the stinky, mind-blowing, sometimes laughable experiences of it all, what remains with me are the great memories of men who became true friends. It was the camaraderie that formed, not only under times of great stress and yes, even fear, but also the comical times that we all shared and remember a lifetime later. Rich men, poor men, white men, black, brown and red men, we were equals during those months and years slogging around in defense of the red, white, and blue. For some of us those lines of culture and nonequity remain nonexistent to this day. That right, David? Ain't that right, Al? You know who you are.

<u>Dan the Soldier Man:</u> Hard to believe I did almost everything but drink out of this helmet. I should have had it bronzed.

<u>Germany, the 595th Signal Company Support:</u> That's me on the left with my buddy Mike, after returning from three weeks in the field. We are showered and ready to have some brews and stir up trouble.

Chapter 8

"If you put a small value upon yourself, rest assured the world will not raise your price."

Anonymous

There were secrets and stories from my time in the service about which I can now laugh, because you had to find humor in it or lose your marbles. We got our jollies where and when we could and we wreaked havoc in between with gusto. We created a new normalcy that worked for us and got us through. Conditioning is an amazing thing.

Although time flies when you are having so much "fun" playing war games, the day came to end my tour and prepare to go home. As part of the protocol I sat in the captain's office in Arkansas and listened to his slippery sales pitch on the benefits of reenlistment. He wrapped it up with a lure that was supposed to make me jump at the chance to stay and wash my butt in my helmet for a few more years. He leaned forward grinning.

"And as an incentive bonus, we will pay you $400 just to reenlist, plus a promotion. Whaddya say?"

I looked him right in the eye and practically spit in his face, "No, sir!"

The smile left his face and he sat back. "Okay, GI, too bad." He got up and left the room.

I didn't think too much about it until I was called back to his office later that afternoon and informed they had "lost" my medical records and my discharge would be delayed by another week. In the meantime, I still belonged to them so they put me on latrine duty and had me cleaning every damn latrine on the post. That was an unsavory result of not taking the "generous" gift of reenlisting. Was it worth it? Hell yes! I was going home sweet home. Finally, I was on a bus heading back to Albuquerque with another soldier I met en route. He was black and I was, well, what was I? Mexican, Hispanic, Latino—whatever. We were both soldiers in uniform heading back to our families. I kept thinking that soon I would be dressed in my civvies with Mom, Dad, my sisters, and my brother, eating tortillas, hot chili and beans. Alleluia! Halfway through Oklahoma we hit a horrific blizzard that just got worse by the mile and visibility was down to almost zero. Eventually the driver told us we would have to get off the highway for safety. There was a roadside diner in a little town not too far ahead where we could pull in, get some hot food, use the facilities, and wait out the storm.

My new buddy and I were hanging back talking while the rest of the civilians piled off the bus and went into the diner for food. Our mouths watering, thinking about hot coffee and some chow, we went in and sat down. After a few minutes we noticed that others were eating and being served, but no one was coming to our table to take our orders. I looked over at my companion and asked, "Hey, they aren't even giving us a glance. What the hell is going on?"

He replied without any emotion, "I guess because I'm a nigger and you're a spic."

My mouth dropped open. "Come on, that can't be." I got up and went up to the counter and asked a guy who seemed to be in charge why we weren't getting service. He gave me the once over, as well as my buddy back at the table, and said loud enough for everyone to hear, "We don't serve the likes of you!"

Holy shit! You are kidding me, right? Immediately, memories surfaced of discriminations from my childhood and I found that I was still embarrassed to my very core. Once again I felt unwanted and unworthy. People were looking at us and I was thinking, *Damn, enough already.* I was so excited to be back in the land of the big "PX" and to be home again with my people. I just needed to get there and into a normal life, if there was such a thing. It took everything I had not to cry right there in the diner because it was so sad, the whole thing was so unbearably sad. This was a piss-ass diner in a piss-ass town full of crazy, prejudiced people. Was there no progress in the country while I was away? Evidently not much from what I could see. It looked like the south had risen again in Oklahoma.

My friend and I could not even use their facilities, but being macho males we knew how to make yellow snow, and we climbed back on the bus. The driver and a couple of passengers inside tried to speak up for us and were told that if they were caught buying food for us they would not be served either. Some, however, figured out how to play dumb and were sneaky enough to get extra food, hide it in their clothing and bring it out. I could tell they felt bad for us and just didn't know what to say. You could see they were deeply ashamed and angry at the actions of their fellow Americans. It was awkward at best.

What I did not expect, and I am sure my black friend did not as well, was what a totally different and radically changed world we were coming back to, as was evident when our bus arrived in Albuquerque. We came back to a world where you now got harassed because you wore a uniform and chose to serve your country. It was a world where it was still not safe to be a minority. My world, to some extent in my mind, was an alien country that I thought I knew but really didn't recognize. This thinking would transform into a deep and abiding anger as my awareness of the many forms of discrimination I was facing dawned on me. And the terrific irony of it all was that down the road I would become a civil rights activist and a long-haired, anti-war hippy.

Eventually I made my way to Mom and Dad's house, excited as hell to see their faces when I showed up unexpectedly on their doorstop. I imagined my mother all teary eyed to have her son back from the army, safe and sound. Then she would gather the family and offer me good food. My taste buds were already juicing up in anticipation. I could hardly wait. I ran up the steps and banged on the door.

That was when I had what I can only define as a Twilight Zone moment. The lady who answered the door was not my mother. When I asked about my parents, she said she thought they had moved to Las Cruces somewhere but did not know the address. I was nauseated, thinking, *Oh God, help me. Help me find my mama. Where are you, Mama?* I was quivering like the little kid who turns around in a crowd and discovers his mother is nowhere to be seen. I had just come from playing war games where I saw a lot of nasty shit, cried a river of tears over the bad stuff and laughed with my buddies because there was nothing else we could do about the situation. I got through all of that, including an appalling and degrading bus ride, and here I was almost bawling on this lady's front walk because I couldn't find my mama.

I shouldered my duffel bag and found a phone where I called my sister-in-law, who thankfully still lived in Albuquerque. When she answered the phone I nearly blubbered into the receiver, "Sis, it's Danny. I'm back."

Then I got the response I craved. "Danny, thank God you're home and you're okay. Mom and Dad will be so happy to see you." I nearly crumbled right there with relief. I made my way to her house, where we called Mom and Dad and let them know that I would soon be on another bus to Las Cruces.

When I arrived there I had the best reception ever, with hugs and tears from my sisters and parents. Even though Mom remarked how handsome I looked in my uniform, I could not wait to get to the bathroom and strip it off and stuff it into my duffel bag. Many years later I pulled the thing out, all wrinkled and musty, and looked at it. I stripped off my sharpshooter medal, one of my nametags, and the chevrons of my rank, and stuffed the rest in my duffel bag, which I did not look at again for decades. Regrettably, I came to find out you can't get rid of memories by stuffing them in a duffel bag. They stay with you, buried in a subconscious file drawer waiting for the day when someone or some event opens the drawer and you discover you aren't as detached from the crap as you thought. Once again you feel the weight of your sadness, guilt, and shame, and wonder at the heaviness of it. And I thought to myself, *How long can I carry this around?* In reality, however, I am still carrying some of the memories along with me, so I guess the answer to the question is a very long time, if you choose to.

On my life journey I saw and experienced quite a bit of the world, storing lots of memories, some quite pleasant, so that bringing them up again was something to enjoy and savor. Others still haunt me with the violence and conflicts that only war can summon. I kept them locked tightly in the back drawer of my mind, but every now and then one would latch on the backside of a good memory and make itself known, spoiling the good stuff for me. It could be argued, however, that there is always violence or a war going on somewhere in the world. I guess it is good for business, profit, and the bottom line—not mine, but someone's.

Many years after my service, I took a trip to Central America, where I was engaged in an "international business" of helping add to someone's bottom line. I recall sitting in a little open patio of a concertina bar, having a brew with a fellow traveler. No uniforms this time. We were taking a break after a visit with an American ambassador. We were chatting it up with the owner of the place where we were staying, a "deluxe" place with no running water, and electricity that only worked until seven o'clock when it was turned off for the night. I nearly choked on my beer when I looked up and there hovering above us was a Russian-made helicopter gun ship with a machine gunner hanging out.

Suddenly all hell broke loose outside and we heard the staccato fire of guns, explosions, and screaming. Then we saw people running all over the place trying to find a place to hide. Just as we were about to ask what was happening, the owner, without missing a beat in his conversation, walked over and closed the double doors that were opened onto the street from the patio area where we were sitting, and asked if we would like another beer. Huh? It was surreal. We just looked at each other for a moment and finally responded with "Yeah sure, why the hell not?" We got kind of punchy and giddy just sitting there, talking and drinking and pretending whatever was happening outside was not happening. The whole thing lasted probably only a few minutes—or an hour. It was hard to tell. Whatever the case, the shooting stopped as abruptly as it started, and the sudden silence was as spooky as the chaos just minutes before.

We got up and cautiously, very cautiously, opened the door and peeked outside. It seemed relatively safe since the gunfire and turmoil had stopped, so I carefully stepped out onto the narrow sidewalk. I walked up the block and what I saw almost made me piss in my pants and I could taste bile at the back of my throat. There was a body of a man lying in the street and, even though he was twenty or thirty feet away, I could see blood flowing from his body into the gutter where it ran right by me not three feet from where I was standing. The blood had turned the dirty water in the gutter to a dark red. I went back inside and had to practically shout at the top of my lungs to get the owner's attention; he seemed totally mesmerized by the gory view. I asked for another beer and chugged the whole thing even though it was warm and tasted sour. My God, when is this stuff going to end? Am I going to make it home in one piece—one piece that is still walking and breathing and not in a pine box?

Another fun moment, same country but a few days later, found me in a pickup out in the backcountry on a Nicaraguan muddy road filled with potholes. I was with a man supposedly on a work sabbatical from an American university and his friend, a young Nicaraguan woman. We were working our way very slowly through the thick jungle when the jungle erupted on both sides of us with guerilla soldiers in camouflage fatigues. They waved at us in a menacing way with their AK-47's and screamed at us in Spanish, "Alto! Alto! Stop! Stop!" They ordered us to get out of the truck and put our hands on our heads. Then they shouted, "Now, now! Move, move!"

The Nicaraguan woman became very indignant and shouted back at them in Spanish to put down their guns while berating them for their actions. I also spoke Spanish and I saw that they did not take well to this mere "woman" telling them what to do. It became apparent to me that this was quickly becoming a dangerous situation and if it continued would not end well for any of us. I reached over and grabbed her, telling her in my most authoritative voice, "Maria, control yourself. We must do what they want." Then I told the guerillas that we meant no harm and they could have all our money, everything we had. In my most deprecating manner I told them we did not mean to take this route; that we did not know it was forbidden to be on this road, blah, blah, blah. I am sure our resident "libber," Maria, must have bitten through her tongue trying to stay quiet and not incite them further, but she did.

The soldiers went off to the side, still pointing their AK-47's at us, and had a little pow-wow with the one who appeared to be the leader. When they came back they waved us on with a warning that the next time we would not be so lucky. As they warned us, they gave Maria unmistakably significant leers that sent chills down my spine. After suppressing a seriously strong urge to throttle Maria, I said a few Hail Mary's of gratitude.

My Central America experience left me with mixed emotions and nightmares that I have to this day even though most of the faces of those I met there have faded. While in Nicaragua I was primarily living in the moment, always watchful, sometimes fearful, scanning the jungles and the skies for the invisible enemy that could show up any time. On the occasions I drove or walked alone through the streets of Managua, I could not help becoming somewhat paranoid when I saw young men on the corners with AK-47's or other weapons hanging from their shoulders.

It felt as if there were eyes and ears everywhere. Was that person watching me watch him? If I had the wrong look on my face, or moved my hand to my pocket in a certain way, would someone think that was a threatening gesture and start firing? You may think I am exaggerating, and maybe I am, but unless you were there you cannot know what it was like. There may be a reason for all this madness, but I have never been able to find it. And after all these years it still has the power to give me night sweats and make my eyes tear up. I rationalize that I was just there doing my job, taking orders, making things happen, and yet for what and for whom? I remember vividly that with all the violence and chaos all I wanted was one thing, the one thing that I prayed for nightly: that God would get me home. Home to be safe, normal Danny again. I knew in my heart that everything would be just perfect as soon as I got home, right?

I will admit even now that there are parts of my life that I will not, cannot, speak of. And I know that every now and then when I am exhausted or my guard is down, something will still trigger a particularly frightening episode and the sweating will start all over again.

A friend of mine once remarked, "Dan, I see you as a basically peaceful warrior, a man who is always striving for peace whether it be in the family or in your community. How did you survive the terror of the atrocities you saw?" I just sat there looking at her, not trusting myself to speak since she had stepped into what I considered to be forbidden territory. My eyes were tearing when she said, "It seems that in order for you to do what you were expected to do and survive, you had to turn your soul off and just get it done."

I had to think about that. Yes, that might be part of it and I also knew in my heart that we all live by choices and once out of the service I chose to do what I did, most likely for all the wrong reasons. I chose to get the job done and did it like a dumbass with gusto so that my "superiors" would look at me and treat me as a "player" in a very spooky, wild, and sometimes violent world. And all the time I was sopping up the praise, I thought myself to be that big player. I was doing some crazy things that very few have done or will ever do. So even though I may have regrets, I acknowledge what I did and accept responsibility for that.

The panic attacks still remind me that wrong reasons are the wrong reasons, no matter what, and it is an ongoing challenge to let it go. Oh, mea culpa! Mea maxima culpa! My friend insisted that I did the best I could with what I had at the time and to use it now as a learning experience. She suggested that I forgive myself, or at least move in that direction, and get on with making a difference in whatever way I can and choose right now. I'm working on it. My mother, my little angel, has seen to that without ever realizing the significant part she played in my healing process.

As the days passed, I watched my sweet mother go deeper into her world of quiet preparation for what was yet to come and I went deeper into my past, digging up memories that brought a flood of emotions—both of us hanging on for dear life.

Chapter 9

"If you don't learn to forgive, those who harmed you or
who don't want peace will control you."

Elza-Lynne Kruger
Cape Town, South Africa

Mom's "war" was getting closer to completion. Who
wins? In some respects she wins because the pain and
suffering will be over. We lose because we watched it and
will lose someone very important to us. We don't want the
suffering to go on—for her or for those who love her and are
conflicted daily over the desire to just want or allow her to go.
War is hell no matter what kind of war. Nobody really wins.

After my return from the service I immediately began the
business of "filing" some of the messy stuff so it would not
haunt me so much. But dreams and exhaustion have a way of
prying open the most airtight of mental safes, and stuff oozed
out at odd hours of the day and night.

I know that my path through life has been strewn with some
roses. There were lots of good times. There were also land
mines lurking under some of those roses. I learned early on
how to sidestep most of them. Piling on more flowers does not
take away the trap underneath. You step on one and it blows up
in your face. What amazed me was my capacity to act shocked
and surprised each time it happened. When I bury something
it no longer exists, right? But where did my emotional wounds
actually have their beginnings, or did they just pile up over
time? Was it in Ely, Nevada? East Los Angeles? Albuquerque?

The military? I think what began as a child just festered little by little each time I felt devalued or negated.

But for now it did not matter because I had just piled on some fresh new roses as I sat, for the moment, an adored son at my mother's home in Las Cruces, New Mexico. I was stuffing my face with tacos when my cousin Steve walked in and asked, "So what are you going to do now, cuz?"

I replied "Don't know, cuz. Probably going to work construction with Bobby, or maybe go back to cutting meat."

Steve looked at me momentarily and asked, "Do you know anything about electronics? You know, about radios and stuff?"

I shook my head. "Not a whole bunch. I was in the Signal Corps, though, and I did carry a radio and I had some training in communications."

Steve went on. "Have you ever thought about working at White Sands Missile Range outside of Las Cruces?" Steve was an Optical Repairman at White Sands and told me about his contacts there. He offered to introduce me. Steve smiled when I looked hopeful. "Who knows, they may help you get a good government job at White Sands."

I got excited. "Yeah, that sounds good. Thanks."

It wasn't long before Steve set up a meeting at his home with George the Electrical Engineer, Joseph the Rocket Scientist, and Pete the Timing and Systems Engineer.

There is a dicho (saying) in Spanish, "Que suerte la mia," which literally translated means "what luck mine." That meeting changed my life course. These wonderful, caring and talented engineers and scientists took this young Latino with no work experience except in construction and meat-cutting and mentored me. They taught me about electronics and helped me enroll at New Mexico State University. Angels can come in many shapes and sizes, so I have heard, and these guys sure fit the criteria for me.

My "angels" set up my interview at White Sands where I would meet Mr. Walters, my future supervisor. After our initial introduction, Walters said to me, "Dan, you have two things against you to get a job here at the Sands. One is that you don't know anything about math and electronics, and the second is you're Mexican and I don't like Mexicans."

I sat there stunned, my mouth went dry, and I think I actually stuttered when I replied, "Sir, I can't do anything about your second concern, but if you give me a chance, I will learn the needed math and electronics and will prove to you I can do a good job here."

He went quiet for a bit while I sat there sweating rings under my armpits. Finally he answered, "Okay, I will give you a six-month trial." Just like that. A potential landmine sidestepped.

My new friends got to work and tutored me until my head was about to burst with new information. Six months later Mr. Walters tested me every which way he could in math and electronics and I demonstrated I could, in fact, do the job. He sat me down, looked me in the eye and said, "Still don't like Mexicans, but you proved you can do the job and you passed the tests so you are hired."

Outside, out of earshot of anyone important, I yelled at the top of my lungs, "YES! YES! I am okay! I am an electronics tech at White Sands Missile Range!" Wow! Later I celebrated with my mentors by buying them all beers. It was difficult to put into words the gratitude I felt. They brushed it off like it was no big deal. "No problem, Dan, we believe you will be a winner someday. You're smart and learn quickly; we're just helping you get started." They were true pioneers, overlooking the color/culture barrier to sponsor a Latino from the 'hood who would go on to become a very successful Latino in a small town along the front range of Colorado. Who knows how many other minorities they helped along the way to success and fulfillment. Oh my! What heart! What caring! What courage! All I can say is God bless them and God bless my cousin Steve who introduced me.

On weekends I would travel the two hundred miles from Las Cruces to Albuquerque to date a gal named Anna who lived there. My Uncle Leo and Aunt Jolie let me bunk with them so I could keep my budding romance going. I thought myself in love with her, but she was into building a career and I thought I should be married. That was the way my culture worked. You got a job, you got married, and you had kids. Anna and I couldn't agree on that so we split up. She later became a rather well-known entertainer and recording artist. I think a little piece of my heart always belonged to her, my first love.

Anna introduced me to Dolores, who lived in the extremely poor Los Barelas barrio. She seemed eager to get hitched and out of there, I was looking for a wife, and after a year of courting, we were married. They say hindsight is 20/20; this event was certainly another life-changer, but more of the disastrous kind.

We bought a little house and were living high on the hog until one day she came to me and said, "Dan, I'm pregnant, and it is not yours. The father is a student at the university here and I need to go somewhere to have the baby and give it up for adoption."

Damn! My new world of success and fulfillment fell apart in an instant. I was so angry and hurt that I could hardly function. Oh God! What now? Oh God, no, please tell me this is not true.

In the ensuing weeks I spent a lot of time alone just sobbing. Finally, I was wrung out, no tears left. I had to make a decision and soon, before people found out about Dolores' dirty deed. I was looking at "help wanted" ads in an El Paso, Texas, newspaper and there was an ad from the Federal Aviation Administration (FAA) advertising the need for people trained in electronics. I thought, *What do I have to lose?* I made an appointment, was interviewed, tested, and hired. Batta bim, batta boom.

We left White Sands—a job I loved—great friends, family, and my mentors. It pained me to lie to them all, telling them I got a much better job with better pay, an advancement opportunity. I felt like such a hypocrite as they all wished me well, congratulating me on my good fortune. Away we went, carrying our "shame" with us to the new job, at a lower payscale at the flight service station in Blythe, California. When Dolores came to term I took her down to San Diego to have the baby and release it for adoption. I told my new colleagues that we took Dolores to San Diego because of the "better" medical facilities but that something went very wrong and the baby died at birth. Now her shame was my guilt, and another landmine that I had to cover up. To this day I hate what I did, but I thought we needed to do it or Dolores would not have been able to face the family. I was also thinking about the shame and embarrassment that might be heaped on me. What a sham! Another big mea culpa, mea maxima culpa for that!

After things settled down a bit, we tucked into life in Blythe. Everyone at my job treated me wonderfully, teaching me what I needed to know to work with the electronics that guided planes across the skies. Later, I was even sent to school at the FAA Academy in Oklahoma City, where I met more interesting people.

Blythe had very few minorities, however, and although we were treated very well, I was still insecure about whether I was welcomed because of the civil rights movement or on my own merits as a human being. In other words, was I being accepted for all the right reasons? I was, after all, still a minority who stood out as a dark Latino among a sea of pale faces. My self-worth still had some growing to do and, looking back, there were many things about this experience that were very enriching. Blythe was a cozy little agricultural town located along the Colorado River. The FAA guys taught me to golf, water ski, took Dolores and me to local restaurants, and generally brought us into their social circle. Things were looking good again.

After a year in Blythe, Dolores informed me she wanted a baby—my baby. Oh boy! My brain was racing. What was she saying? Was she setting the stage to tell me she was unfaithful again. What the hell! Not again! Never again! But after a lot of talking she convinced me she really had seen the error of her ways and was ready to start a family of our own.

Celia, my CC, was born ten months later in Las Cruces, where Dolores went to be with my family when her time came. I cannot describe the feeling of holding my little daughter in my arms for the first time. She was a real beauty and had a little dimple on her chin. We called her "CC" in honor of me, my father, and my grandfather. Much later, when our beautiful Elaine was born, I realized that I would never have any treasure greater in worth than my two daughters.

Back in Blythe we were congratulated on how lucky we were that this baby had lived since our "son" had not. That reopened the ol' can of worms about giving up the baby, who could be living within a couple hundred miles of us for all we knew. I also noticed that Dolores began to change, becoming despondent and unhappy. We were living amongst our lies again and it was not helping the relationship. She started coming up with excuses to leave, like our place was too small, not nice enough for CC, and so on.

Finally Dolores told me we had to move—for CC's sake. Well, the ghosts were getting to me too, so we decided that we would start looking around for another opportunity elsewhere. One of my secret goals was to be back in Colorado, so I watched FAA opportunities in that region. In the meantime, I kept up with my job, and my occasional lengthy trips to the FAA Academy kept my training up to par. Because the baby was so small and Dolores was not comfortable being alone, I took her back to Las Cruces to be with my family during one of these trainings. It was one to remember, most definitely.

On this training, I arrived in Oklahoma City on a Friday evening in late summer. My wife and baby were safe at my mom's house for the duration of this training that would last a few months. I checked into a local hotel, got some sleep, and the next morning around noon I went to check out the pool. There was only one person there and he was sitting by the edge of the pool drinking Coors beer from a case he had next to him. Like the wise ass I was, I asked him jokingly, "You gonna drink that all by yourself?"

He looked up at me and drawled, "What's that? And who the hell are you? Look, it's my beer so stuff it!" I backed off and apologized, at which point he offered me a beer. So I got me a Coors from the case, slipped into the pool, and we started having small talk.

During our conversation I kept thinking, *I have seen this dude before, but where?* When I could not figure it out I finally said to him, "I think I have seen you before, like I know you from somewhere."

He looked at me with an odd, disgusted look and said, "Really? You think you know me? What a half-assed way of recognizing me. Big deal!"

I really felt stupid because it dawned on me who he was. "You're with Elton John, aren't you?" I asked.

He said, "Ya think? Come on, you knew all the time who I was; you were just trying to be cool. What you look like is stupid." Well, I did feel a bit stupid, but somehow, with the beers and all, we got past that and went on talking like "cool dudes" and drinking Coors till we finished the whole case. We were feeling no pain when he asked me, "You want to be my 'Scotch six-pack guy' at the concert this evening?"

He didn't have to twist my arm. Oh, hell yes. He told me I would be carrying a six-pack of Johnny Walker Scotch for the group and keeping it ready back stage for the band. I was to be out front at six. You betcha. At six o'clock, a black stretch limo pulled up, I climbed in the back, and he handed me a carton with six bottles of Johnny Walker Scotch, saying nothing more. We arrived at the concert hall and I got out, walking behind the entourage with the Scotch as all the fans waved and hooted at the stars in front of me. Of course I waved back just like I was a member of the band. This Latino boy was having a hell of a rush!

After the concert I climbed back into the limo and was let out in front of the hotel with instructions to go to their suite for a private party if I wanted to. Are you kidding me, of course I wanted to. I was IN, baby!

I sat at the party in total awe. Music blaring full blast, booze flowing, women cavorting around, and general bedlam all around me. Everyone seemed pretty blasted, but the big man himself, the star of the hour, was sitting in his shorts in the middle of the huge bed reading a book, calm as could be, seemingly oblivious to all the chaos around him. It was weird. Later on I found myself wandering along the street pretty smashed, not believing what had happened to me over the past twenty-four hours. It was one of my "Danny's crazy moments to remember." Dolores had trouble believing me when I bragged about it. She may have been a bit jealous. I would have been.

After my return to Blythe from the FAA Academy, when CC was nine months old, Dolores hit me with, "Dan we are going to have another baby?"

My eyes popped. "What, for real?" She said it was definite, and this time one hundred percent of me had no doubt that this was our baby. She started in on me again about how we needed to move so I started searching more earnestly among the FAA job bids. Within a couple of days I saw a bid for a radar technician at the new FAA Air Route Traffic Control Center (ARTCC) in Longmont, Colorado.

I looked it up on the map and saw it was about 30 miles north of Denver. My uncle, aunt and my brother lived in Denver and I thought, "Wow, this could be it!" Even though I was not radar trained I bid on the job because it might get me back in Colorado.

Unfortunately, I did not inform my boss, Mr. Jones, that I was applying for another post. Part of me did not think I would get it anyway, but when he found out about it through the regional office he was really upset. It was not a pretty scene in his office. Here was a man who went above and beyond to help me out, provided me training, brought me into the social fold, and consoled me when we "lost" our baby. He told me how much he counted on me to be part of their team and felt like he had been blindsided without so much as a word from me. Man! I told him that my wife wanted to be near family, and my family was back in Colorado. After more berating about how I was bailing out on him and the team, he reluctantly gave in and said he would give me the recommendation I needed.

I left there with my tail between my legs, feeling like a real turncoat. Once again I was hopping through hoops for Dolores and, I hoped, my babies. That is what we Latino men do: whatever is necessary to keep their families together. I felt like I had no real control over my life. It was now spinning around me with Dolores as the captain. Although it sounded good to be moving back near my own family, I had built a good reputation and circle of friends in Blythe who I would miss very much.

I shed some rather unmanly tears under a shade tree before I went home to tell Dolores that I got the job. Once I informed Dolores where Longmont, Colorado, was, she wanted to start packing immediately so we could get on the road to the "promised land."

Little did I know that the paradise I envisioned in Longmont would turn out to be another horrible lesson in racial discrimination, one that would last years. And somewhere in those years, I would be left to raise my daughters alone. Adios, Blythe dream. Hola, Longmont nightmare.

Chapter 10

"A sure way to lose happiness, I found, is to want it
at the expense of everything else."

Bette Davis

We arrived in the charming city of Longmont, Colorado,
in spring in the early '60s. Both Dolores and I marveled at
the idyllic setting of this place against the backdrop of the
mountains. I thought maybe this would finally make her
happy and more secure. My aunt and uncle graciously invited
us to stay with them in Denver until we found our own place
in Longmont.

I was eager to begin my new career at the Denver Air
Route Traffic Control Center and dug right in getting trained
and meeting my new colleagues. That part went really well and
I applied myself to the next process of finding us a nice house
to rent. We wanted to settle into our new little community as
quickly as possible.

I was totally unprepared for what happened next, although
you would think I would have known these things by now.
We looked all through Longmont and saw a lot of nice places
until we found a sweet little house for rent on Sunset on the
west side of town near the local golf course. We thought this
might be a perfect place for our family. I located a local real
estate agent and asked about the house. I was treated to one
of my déjà vu moments when I was told, "That won't work
because your kind lives only on the east side. Let me show
you some places over there."

"Our kind"? I think both our mouths dropped open, and I remember an awkward silence until I finally managed to croak, "Okay, show us some houses on the east side."

We followed him, like little puppies that had been properly chastised, to Kensington Avenue, where we did find a house we could rent. Score: Prejudice, one; Dan and Dolores, zero.

I learned later that this was actually the norm for "people of color," but damn, to be forced to live on the "other side of the tracks," taking away my freedom to choose—huh uh. My white counterparts at traffic control making the same money as I did could live where they chose, and none of them as I recall chose the east side. This new beginning in the "Promised Land" was not very promising, and Dolores was getting close to giving birth to our second daughter. Keeping her calm took a lot more energy and time than I had to spare at this point. I was angry beyond reckoning but had to make a huge effort to appear calm, for CC and Dolores. I wasn't going to make any waves, not now anyway.

We settled into our new house and, shortly thereafter, our beautiful Elaine came into the world. They held her up so I could see her through the nursery glass and I marveled at her little face. Once again I thought to myself, "Que suerte la mia." What luck mine. And Longmont United Hospital did not have a "color barrier"; we were treated like everyone else. Thank God for small blessings.

Shortly after Elaine's birth, Dolores became restless again. "We have two daughters now, we need a better place, you have a good job, and we should be able to afford it." She would not let it go and the incident around the Sunset house was still grating on her so she bugged me incessantly with things like, "Please, Dan, please. If you love us you will make them rent us a place as nice as that house on Sunset. We are good people and you work at an important job at the FAA."

Okay, already, I gave in and went out searching. It turned out that the house on Sunset was still available, and this time I gathered my courage, stepping into unknown territory, namely the "west side" and approached the owner directly.

I put on my best 'white Latino' act and, after a lot of negotiations, the owner finally agreed to give us a chance. All right! I was so high I could hardly stand it. Dolores would be so happy and my girls would have a nice place to live. We moved over to the west side. I thought I had arrived.

Looking back, I believe we were the first "people of color" to move into the "white west." I also know that I did a lot of bowing and backside-kissing to be allowed to live and play in a part of the community that was previously closed to "my kind." Back then I felt I was doing what I had to do to be the equal of those pale faces around me and be accepted into their ranks. Sunset Street was a damn good start, wasn't it? The good part was it looked like I was the carrier of the proverbial torch, breaking new ground for others to follow.

In reality, I wanted to be like them, not like me, whoever that was. Yeah, yeah, for all the wrong reasons, I know that now. I thought acceptance was what I wanted and damn the expense. I had huge self-worth issues to deal with and this was my way of dealing. Getting to the west side was a temporary fix for a deeper scar that had not really healed, but having ignited the torch, I'd illuminated the shadows. Life sent me a couple of earth angels to help light the way, but not without some "gifts" of opportunity to test me big time!

I got to know my buddies at the FAA and hung out with them when I could. Many of them belonged to private clubs like the Elks and Moose lodges, and sometimes they would take me as their guest on days off to play pool and drink some brews. It was a great stress reliever from the air traffic control environment that can be intense at times. Some of my closest friends were members of the local Elks and I really enjoyed hanging out with them.

One day my friend Ray came up to me and said, "You know, Dan, it doesn't make sense that you keep coming as my guest to the Elks. Since you seem to enjoy it, why don't

I sponsor you for membership? Then you can come and go whenever you want to?" Oh man, I was going to be an Elk, a member of a private club. I pumped Ray's hand and nodded my head with a huge smile that could have cracked my face from ear to ear.

The Elks. Now that was meaningful and symbolic in many ways to me. My mind raced back to a time when Bobby and I were kids and went out hunting with Dad. On those special, chilly, pre-dawn mornings we would load up on a hearty breakfast of tortillas, chili, eggs, and crisp bacon, and then head out with Dad. We loved gum and there wasn't always money for store-bought gum so we would go out in the woods looking for just the right pine tree that was oozing just the right pinesap. We would grab a bit, roll it between our fingers, and chew on it like a resin-flavored piece of Juicy Fruit, without the fruit and without much juicy. Then we would hunker in behind Dad as he hunted the big elk, sometimes crawling painfully on our hands and knees through the low brush. With his trusty 30-30 rifle, he would slowly get a bead on a big ol' stag and bring him down, usually with one shot.

For two little boys these creatures seemed like behemoths, giants of the forest. We were like apprentices, too, as we observed and listened while Dad taught us how to cut the animal's throat to drain the blood, remove the scent glands, gut it from stem to stern and then gawked in total awe when he reached inside and carefully pulled out the innards and entrails carefully saving the liver for a special meal that Mom would prepare. For us that was a gourmet banquet, rare and exciting. Then came the best part: Dad would carefully pry open the elk's mouth and, with the precision of a surgeon, extract the white ivory molars. These were highly sought after by members of the Elks Club in Trinidad, who made watch fobs out of them. Dad got five dollars per molar and the money from those teeth was more than he made all month on the ranch. Dad considered our hunting expeditions another one of our rituals of making boys into men.

I fingered the smooth molar that I still carried around with me. Dad gave it to me a lifetime ago, a precious gift, and I carried it still, a reminder of the man who struggled to provide for his family, the man who told me to become something better. Well, Dad, I was doing my best and this looked like I was almost there. The Elks. Wow!

Early one Saturday morning I heard a knock on my door and there was my buddy Ray, my wonderful sponsor. I got excited. This was it! I invited him in and tried to be cool.

"Ray, mi amigo, come in. I know it's early but would you like a beer?" I didn't notice at the time that Ray was kind of fidgeting by the door. I went on like a blithering fool, "You come to tell me the good news, did you? Sit down, sit down."

Ray looked really uncomfortable now. "No, Dan. I don't know how to tell you this, but the answer is, no." I thought he was kidding me, building up to the big moment. Then Ray sat down and beckoned me to join him. I asked him what happened and that is when he hit me with the real news.

"Dan, you've been blackballed."

What did he say? Blackballed? Here in America we should be past this crap, right? I thought we were making progress here in Longmont, at least, but nope, same ol', same ol'. I must have looked like I was expecting Ray to suddenly jump up, slap me on the back, and say he was pulling my leg.

"Nope, Dan, this is no joke. They really did blackball you and I can't tell you how mad this makes me." Again he must have sensed what was on my mind because he nodded and said it was because I was Mexican and they did not allow Mexicans in the club. Another punch in the gut by the hard, right hook of prejudice.

I was trying to take it and be stoic about it but my face showed my misery. I wasn't sure whether to cry or hit something. Ray stood up and put his hand on my shoulder. He told me he and his buddies were willing and ready to walk out of the Elks as a protest, sending a strong message that they would not tolerate this shit, not here, not now. I put on a brave face. "No, Ray, you and the guys really like going there. You don't have to do that for me."

The local Elks not only did not allow Mexicans, they did not allow anyone of color. I just happened to be the first Mexican to apply that I knew of. My idyllic town just dropped a bunch of notches and my compass just swiveled from its east-west orientation to a north-south direction, and a deep south at that.

Once again an earth angel appeared in the guise of George, the Grand Exalted Ruler of the Elks. When he heard what had happened, he contacted me. He went on to explain that he was ashamed and embarrassed by what some of his members had done and, as the Grand Exalted Ruler, he was going to use that position to end this madness. He personally sponsored me and waited until only those who he knew would vote for me showed up and, voila, I was in.

Shortly after he gave me the good news he provided a word of caution. "Dan, when you show up for the first time to use your membership, promise me that you will behave like Gandhi, no matter what." I was not really sure what he meant by "a Gandhi." He warned that I might be tested by a few and how I acted or overreacted could make the difference whether I would have an easy membership or a hard one. What the hell? Now I had to stay below the radar on my approach to the runway just to prove myself to these blinkered rednecks! Nevertheless, I promised George that I would do as he requested.

I got my chance soon enough when I went, as a proud new member, to the Elks for the first time to have a drink after work. I was sitting there enjoying myself over a cold one thinking so far so good. This wasn't bad at all. Maybe those guys decided to just let it be. Yeah, right. Next thing I knew I was looking up at a paunchy redneck who leered at me while pouring a beer over my head.

"Go away. You don't belong in our club. Get out." He had a couple of friends who were laughing. Others around just dropped their heads, embarrassed, including me.

Every fiber of my being wanted to spring off that stool and tear into the guy. He had a couple of buddies with him, but I had a lifetime of built-up rage from assholes like that and I was ready to let him have all of it right then and there.

Then I remembered George and my promise to him. He had stepped out on a huge limb to get me here and I owed him big time. Okay, Gandhi, here's to looking full on at the reality of the saying, "An eye for an eye only ends up making the whole world blind." This was a precedent-setting moment and I was, whether I liked it or not, setting the vision for those who would follow me. I was also accepting some responsibility for restoring the sight of two-legged donkeys wearing blinkers. I hung onto my seat as if stuck there with glue, just breathing in and out, in and out, until the guys figured out that they looked more stupid than I did (or at least I hope they did) and left.

Once again I thanked the courage of Ray, George, and my friends who stood up for me helping to put the first big crack in a system that needed some demolition and change. Bless them. This time they were the torchbearers. My role was to keep their flame burning brightly. Together we would light up this beautiful town of Longmont, hopefully, without blinding the newly sighted!

Not used to my Ghandi role, I still wasn't sure whether I was really courageous or just plain stupid. Sometime later I talked to Mama about it. I told her how much it hurt and asked if it was always going to be like that. Was I right or was I wrong not to fight back? What hurts them so bad that they feel that they have to hurt me in order to heal it? I wanted some acknowledgement for being the first to break the Elks' color barrier with this nonviolent, Gandhi approach.

Just like Mama, she gave me what I craved. "Hijo, I know you did the right thing for the right reasons. I am very proud of you. By you being humble and taking the hurt, you helped them heal their pain; you are the one who is now free."

Wow, Mama had just turned "being humble" into a weapon and not the "low self-worth" cross that I had been bearing!

She'd healed my wound and freed me of both "self-doubt" as well as the pain. Martin Luther King's liberating chant, "Free at last, free at last, thank God Almighty, we are free at last!" pounded through my mind, and my heart soared.

I don't remember now but Mama probably also offered me chili and tortillas to calm me down. That's sort of like Mexican chicken soup for the soul. Ah, I could always count on her, my first and best earth angel.

Chapter 11

"Sólo el que carga el morralito sabe cuanto pesa
(only he who carries the knapsack knows
how much it weighs)."

Mexican Proverb

So we were living large in Longmont, finally. The FAA was treating me well and the moolah was coming in to the extent that we bought a sweet tri-level on Sumac Street. We were homeowners. Things should be happy inside the Benavidez house, right?

Nope. No racial issues at this point, but the home front was once again rocky. Not that it was ever really smooth. I tried to give Dolores everything she needed within my power, but it was never enough. Although we did not really argue much, her mood swings were becoming more frequent and intense.

She was definitely troubled and her highs and lows were rollercoaster extremes. I was unhappy and worried about Dolores, and our daughters who were living in this up-and-down circus not understanding what was happening to their mother. Sometimes I thought she felt out of her league among our newly formed upscale social set because she came from the poorest of the lowest barrio located next to the sewage treatment plant in Albuquerque. With no real family except a mother with whom she had little contact and a father who was institutionalized, she was totally unprepared for this lifestyle and, perhaps, life in general. And she was the one who insisted on a nicer neighborhood, in a nicer house with "respectable" friends. Perhaps she was overwhelmed, and perhaps there was some genetic predisposition to mental illness. I did not know for sure and we had little awareness about these things at the time. I, for one, was very busy climbing the "white ladder" of success. I had already crossed the west side living barrier and then the Elks. What next? I was fairly comfortable at this stage with mixing it up with the upper echelons, but I don't think Dolores was.

It was later in my life that I realized my responsibility for part of her problem. Ah, there's that hindsight vision again that brings such wisdom after the fact. In looking back I saw that I did not truly understand her needs and the tremendous amount of support she required. I came from a culture that believed and practiced the "old way" where a woman's place was in the home raising the children, tending the house, and her husband. I did not include her in my inner thoughts and feelings and all the external things happening to me outside our home. It was a time of change with regards to women's rights and I was not hip on that particular arena of discrimination. In some ways I was treating her like an object, not a wife and life partner. At the time I thought to myself, "What the hell is the matter with her? Why isn't she happy?" After all, I was making good money, I provided a good house, and food and clothing for her and our daughters. What more did she want? Oh yeah, Dan, lots of learning there. Those wrong reasons just kept piling up. Many good things came out of my efforts, and along with them some not so good. But you are never too old to learn, right? Hope so.

As the months wore on, Dolores became more manic-depressive. There were more frequent nights that she would simply go missing and I had no idea where she was. I became so anxious that I would sneak out on my break when I worked the night shift, running home to see if Dolores was there or had gone out and left my daughters alone. I began having little panic attacks of my own. After a while others knew, but did not speak openly of it to me, that Dolores was mentally "out on the town," so to speak. She would get in one of her manic modes and go out partying with her friends, some of them wives of friends of mine, coming home all happy and loving. These episodes would be followed by the big depressions where she didn't care whether she dressed, ate, or if the girls were taken care of properly.

It got so bad that one of the wives suggested she seek professional help. I was ready to try anything. This was not something I could fix. Upon a recommendation from a "friend," Dolores found a psychiatrist in Boulder and began to have regular visits with Dr. "Joe."

I thought, *She is in professional hands, it will be okay now.* Never in my wildest dreams did I think that a "sick" situation could actually get sicker. I remember how very surprised and flattered I was when Dr. Joe invited us to a party at his fancy house in Sunshine Canyon near Boulder, Colorado. Looking back, however, I should have refused. I did think it kind of odd that he would invite one of his patients to a personal social gathering. But Dolores was flattered and all gaga about her new doctor, so I thought, *Why not?* More mingling with the rich and influential and it might even help my social standing to meet some new people. How could it hurt? It was much later that I realized all this was the beginning of the end for Dolores.

I'm not sure whether I was naïve or simply stupid thinking I would benefit by hobnobbing with those I thought to be bigwigs. Dr. Joe's parties were notorious in some circles. Depending on who you were, you were either flattered or repulsed by one of his invitations. At the time we fit into the former category. (Yeah, yeah, all wrong, I know.) Once we arrived and were introduced to the other guests, the "doc" put drinks in our hands and told us to enjoy. Looking back, I am wondering why he did not offer any warnings about my wife drinking while taking meds he prescribed. He also did not offer any warnings as, unbeknownst to me, he dropped some acid into my drink as a big practical joke.

I knew I was in deep shit the moment I finished my drink. It hit me really hard. Other than booze, I had never imbibed in drugs or hallucinogens of any kind. I began hallucinating immediately and I felt I was in a 3-D walking nightmare.

I had to get out of there and I was trying to round up Dolores and leave. When we were getting ready to leave I could hear the doc's wife hollering at him, "What the hell did you do to him, damn you! You drugged him didn't you? Go get him something now! I mean now!"

The doc's face looked all "warpy" to me, like some weird gargoyle, and he was laughing and saying it was just a joke, no big deal, and he would give me some suppositories to help. Then he hugged Dolores and told her she better drive. Well duh.

For over a month I could barely function. I was a paranoid mess, especially at nights when I would find myself balled up in a fetal position battling night sweats and dreams that left me so wrung out that I was pretty much a half-functioning zombie at work. My buddies kept asking what was wrong and I kept saying I did not feel good and I had some bug that just wouldn't go away. It wasn't far from the truth. It was like a parasite was eating away at my sanity.

When Dolores saw that I was not recovering from the acid she recommended, actually insisted, I see Dr. Joe since he was doing "wonders" with her. Looking at these written words I have to laugh at myself. Go back to the asshole who did this to me? Well, yes, I did for one visit. All he said was, "Dan, you are not crazy, it's just the residual acid moving out of your system. It may take you more time since you seem to be more susceptible than most." Y'think? I was half-expecting him to advise me to take one "acid aspirin" and call him in the morning.

Now I not only had low self-esteem issues, I could add complete stupidity to my list. Except for an unstable wife who could not love anything and the fact that I was more or less permanently affected by my one experience with acid, I was

almost the perfect Latino male: married, kids and a good job.
Take what you can get, Danny.

Although Dolores was devoted to Dr. Joe and was keeping
up with her visits, her illness continued to worsen. She was in
and out of the psych ward and had several failed attempts at
suicide. What was driving this torment of hers?

She would not talk to me at all, and could barely look at
me most of the time. I know her background and genetics may
have played a significant role, but I did have a rather large
"A-ha!" moment when I finally discovered that not long after
she started treatment she and the good doctor began a torrid
affair that lasted a very long time. By my speculation, she and
her "therapist" had most likely been entangled when old Joe
decided to drop some goodies in my drink. Practical joke, my
ass. Perhaps the doc needed some intense therapy himself, or
a refresher course on moral ethics. Or, and I liked this idea the
best, maybe a good ass-whoopin'.

Dolores eventually spent more time away from home and
more time in Boulder. Mama came to stay with me off and on
to take care of Elaine and Celia. I was heartbroken and getting
more and more depressed and confused about Dolores.

One night I had just finished a mid-shift at the Center
and could not wait to get home and get some much needed
sleep. Knowing that Mama would be there taking care of
things allowed me to just relax a bit. Before I hit the bed
I decided that since I had not heard from Dolores in over a
week, I would try calling her good friend, Jane, to see if she
had heard from or seen her lately. She told me she had not
seen Dolores in a couple of weeks. Ah well, not the first time
she had disappeared, so I crashed for about five hours.

When I got up, I went to pick up the mail and found
a huge, ugly surprise on my Visa bill. It was loaded with
charges from, of all places, New Orleans! What the hell
was that about? I knew it had to be Dolores, so I called Jane
again. She had heard that Dolores went to New Orleans with
another "friend." Huh? I asked Jane who the friend was,

and after some hemming and hawing, Jane said most likely her "doctor friend."

Man! Would this never end? I knew she was falling apart and now I was as well. Other than the credit card, she had no money, no job, just the "good doc" to take care of her. What about the kids? How could she simply walk away from her daughters? I tried to remind myself that I loved her. I still loved her, right? It obviously wasn't enough. Mom found me crying over the Visa bill and simply put her arms around me.

"Don't cry hijo, don't cry. We will figure this out. I am here with you and the girls. Things will be all right."

What would I have done without her there? I shudder to think. What strength she had and she gave plenty of it to me and to my girls.

Two weeks later, I was once again coming home from a mid-shift, tired and looking for a beer and some rest. I walked into my house and there was Dolores with the girls and my mom all standing in the living room as if everything was normal.

I started right in on her. "My God! Where have you been? What is wrong with you! What's going on? Dammit, Dolores, please tell me what is happening?"

She looked at me very calmly, at least for her, and said she was unhappy and was leaving for good. When I asked her why, all she could say over and over was, "I just have to."

My stomach in knots, I asked her, "What about Elaine and Celia? If you go, they stay with me and Mama."

I thought that might shake her up, but all she said in return was, "Oh, that's okay. I want your mama to be their only mama from now on." I practically begged her. I told her how bad I felt for letting her down and anything I might have done to hurt her, but she simply looked at me with a haunted look in her eyes and said, "No, Dan, it's not you, it's me. You have nothing to feel guilty about."

I asked her how she was going to get to wherever she was going. She just shook her head and said she would find a way. I knew where she was going before I asked. She got all teary-eyed and said she was going to Boulder to give me time to sort all this out and would be back in a couple of days. *You have GOT to be kidding me,* I thought.

About a week later she returned to say that she was definitely leaving and advised me to go ahead with divorce proceedings. There wasn't anything she wanted as far as any of our assets so it should be easy. Easy?! Out the door she went and I sat down on the couch with my head in mi mamacita's lap blubbering like a little boy. I was grateful the girls were not there to see that.

A few months later the divorce was finalized. All Dolores said she wanted was the assurance that the girls would be taken care of. We stood there in our living room one last time just staring at each other. Then I lost it and put my arms around her. I did not know what else to do. I gave her the car and $300, the only cash I had, to help her get to wherever she was going with whomever she was going. She started crying and hugged me hard, and then walked out of the house and my life. I found out later she was heading to North Carolina with Doctor Joe. What I did not know was that was the last time I would ever see her alive.

Mama, the girls, and I eventually settled into a routine that seemed to work for us considering everything that had happened. I was working, keeping up my relationships with my buddies, and looking to move on. I came home one day after one of those quick "turnaround shifts" tired but feeling pretty good. I had a nice dinner with Mom and my girls and we talked about what went on in their day. About seven I excused myself to go lay down for a bit and read.

I must have dozed off because the ringing of the phone woke me at 9:00. I was a bit groggy when I answered the phone. The person on the other end of the line asked, "Is this Dan Benavidez?" I responded in the affirmative, wondering if this was a sales call. It was not.

The disembodied voice said, "Dan, this is 'Doctor Joe' calling from North Carolina and I have some very bad news.

I hate to be the one to tell you this, but Dolores was killed today. The worst part is my son killed her. He accosted her in a parking lot, they had an argument, and he beat her to death with a rock." Then there was silence.

What?! I said something like, "Is this another of your sick jokes? What the hell are you telling me?" The good doctor responded simply, "No, Dan, it's true, and I will contact you again when I have more details." Then he hung up on me. The doc's son? It seems me and my girls were not the only ones affected by the entanglement of Doctor Joe and Dolores. It was beyond sad. It was insane.

I sat on the stairs in shock, wondering how I would tell my girls, now 12 and 13, that their mother was dead and the horror of how she died. Oh God, please help me on this one! I decided to wait until morning, which was Saturday, to tell the girls.

Next morning, the girls got up and were just sitting down to eat one of Mom's great breakfasts when I walked in and asked them all to come to the family room because I needed to talk to them. Celia looked up.

"Okay, Dad, but I'm hungry. Can it wait until after breakfast?" Mom reminded me that the breakfast would get cold if we interrupted it now. I looked at Mom. "I know Mom, but please, let's all go into the family room. This is very important and it cannot wait."

Mom could see by my face that something was up so she herded the girls into the family room where we all sat on the couch. It was then I started to cry. Alarmed, Celia asked, "Dad, why are you crying. What's wrong?"

I looked at them, trying hard not to totally break down. "I have some bad news about your mother."

They looked at me quizzically and almost in unison said "What's wrong, Dad? Just tell us."

I found I could hardly speak when I told them, "Your mother is dead. I got a call a little while ago from Dr. Joe in North Carolina and he told me she is dead."

After the first shock of what I said settled, Elaine asked, "Dad, how did she die? Tell us. Please tell us."

I'd gone over this a thousand times about how I could soften the blow on the details. And they deserved the truth. They knew about their mother's antics and her problems and had to live through it with me. I chose the simple truth.

"Dr. Joe, who as you know is now married to your mother in North Carolina, called and told me his son, Jimmy, killed her after an argument they had."

Celia immediately screamed, "No! No! No! No!" Elaine looked stunned for a moment, and then joined her sister screaming and shaking their heads in disbelief. Mama sat there, her face white with shock. We had to reaffirm over and over that their mother was really gone. Even though they saw very little of Dolores, she was still their mother. They insisted on knowing everything I knew and I reluctantly told them. All of us huddled together on the couch while Mama and I did our best to reassure our girls that we loved them and that we were a strong family and we would get through this together. I told them again and again how much I loved them and that I was there for them. We wrapped our arms around each other sharing our grief, each of us wondering the same thing. Why? Good God Almighty, what next? What next? Enough already!

Sometime later CC—Celia—found out through a mutual friend that Jimmie (the doc's son) had been tried and convicted of murder and sent away for life to the state penitentiary. I remember her looking at me and commenting, "It is the very least he deserves for killing my mother."

A year had passed when CC and I met up with our friend Jane, who dropped another bombshell on us. It seemed that Jimmy could not deal with either his incarceration or the weight of what he had done, or both, because he committed suicide.

CC had mixed emotions, as did I. I remember her looking at me. "Dad, I guess I should be glad that he is gone since he killed my mommy, but it is so gross and sad and horrible. Why do I feel so bad?"

I gathered my daughter in my arms to console her as best I could. Was it now over? Who won? No one from my observation. Two families were left torn apart and were grieving over the loss of a loved one. Losses that might have been prevented in my view.

I wonder what the good doctor is doing these days? How is he dealing (or not) with his share of the responsibility in the deaths of two people, one a son and the other a former patient who trusted him completely? Only God and the doc know the answer to that one.

As for me and my family, we were busy trying to pull the pieces back together and move forward as best we could into some state of normalcy, whatever that meant.

Chapter 12

"What you need to know about the past is that no matter
what has happened, it has all worked together to bring
you to this very moment. And this is the moment
you can choose to make everything new."

Anonymous

It was my watch again, time with Mom. I looked over
at my sleeping angel and realized that her impending demise
was bringing me more in touch with my own mortality,
which in some mysterious way was a catalyst for all these
unstoppable flashbacks.

I was well aware for some time, many years actually, of
Latino minority tensions simmering just beneath the surface
in our town. We were not alone; it was spreading along the
front range of Colorado. It was more visible to us because of
the nature of our community, its agricultural background and
the larger number of Latinos living here. For some reason
it seemed amplified here, perhaps because of our size. Yes,
indeed, there was a racial volcano building, and it would
not take much to blow the top off. And that pressure was
becoming unbearable as the racial inequalities made the
rift between our local government, the police and private
businesses widen.

I have vivid memories, as do others older than me, of
having to stand at the back of a line to get service at stores,
or signs in windows that read, "No Dogs, No Mexicans."
There was even a time when our city was pretty much run

by the Ku Klux Klan. Now that I think back on it, or perhaps without realizing it, that volcanic pressure was building inside of me as well.

It seemed fitting that the catalyst would occur close to midnight on a hot, muggy August night. According to the public records, a twenty-two-year-old rookie cop was traveling north on Main on his way home for dinner when he noticed a fellow officer arguing with the driver of a car he had pulled over for expired plates. Smoke was coming out of the bottom of the car. Thinking his fellow officer might need backup, he pulled up behind the first officer and got out of his car.

At that moment a Chevy Monte Carlo drove by with five people in it, four of them Latinos. They slowed down and a white male rolled down his window and shouted, "Fuck you, pigs!" The officer writing the ticket yelled back to the rookie officer just arriving, "Go after them and ticket them!" Oh my, things were about to become undone in tranquil Longmont.

The rookie turned on his flashing lights and siren and took off after the Monte Carlo and pulled them over. When he approached the car and peered into the interior, he noticed a white male who appeared to be slightly intoxicated. He shouted into the car, "I want to talk to the loudmouth."

The white man got out of the car but refused to provide his name. Tensions escalated when two of the Latino male passengers, Garcia and Cordova, jumped out of the car, intending, by all accounts, to "help" their buddy. Their first mistake was getting out of the car. The second was opening their mouths. Approaching the cop, they shouted, "You're not taking our friend! No way you're going to do this!"

The rookie took a step back as a precaution. By this time, the first officer, who had finished with the car with expired plates, was arriving on the scene. Sensing an opportunity, the white male ran. The arriving cop took off after him, tackling and throwing him to the ground as the white guy screamed, "Police brutality!"

The rookie, who had pulled the Monte Carlo over, ran to help. He pulled the struggling white man up and pinned him against the police cruiser. As he did, he noticed the two young Latino males who had gotten out of the car approaching the other officer, who immediately got into a physical struggle with Garcia. Afraid Garcia was trying to get the other officer's gun, the rookie released the white guy and went to help. Garcia separated from the officer and bent down to pick up the officer's flashlight that had fallen to the ground. The rookie, thinking it was his buddy's gun, pulled his revolver and fired at Garcia, hitting him in the chest and killing him.

Just as the rookie fired, he heard another gun go off. His fellow officer was on his knees. The rookie thought Cordova must have shot him. In fact, the other officer's gun had accidentally discharged into the air in the struggle. Cordova, probably scared shitless by the gunfire and seeing Garcia bleeding, attempted to escape across the road. The rookie claimed that Cordova was turning around with his arms out. Because he thought Cordova had just shot the other officer and was now turning a "gun" on him, the rookie leaned over the hood of his cruiser and fired at Cordova, dropping him in the road with a wound that would prove fatal. As it turned out Cordova's wound was in the back.

The reality was that Cordova and Garcia had no weapons. And the one who started it all was, ironically, the white male who shouted, "Fuck you, pigs!"

In less than a minute on a steamy August night, an undertrained, stressed-out rookie white cop overreacted and two young Latinos were dead. More than twenty years later, the officer who fired those killing shots expressed in an interview for the local newspaper, "I needed to be in command of it from the opening bell and I wasn't. Experience gives you that, and I didn't have any of that."

Yes, change was coming to our tranquil community and nothing would ever be the same. Not for the town of Longmont and certainly not for me. The volcano was beginning to spew.

It was on that same muggy Friday night, the 14th of August 1980, that I became part of either the problem or solution, depending on your perspective. Either way, my life changed again and my destiny took a hard right turn.

I remember it was a particularly hot August exacerbated by an unusually large infestation of miller moths that descended upon our town in late spring and hung around longer than was usual. It seemed you could not open your mouth without gagging on one of the furry, dusty things. Up in my bedroom that night, I lay sweating and dozing, trying to breathe as little as possible in the still heat, waking up every so often to the thump and crunch of some bastard moths hitting the blades of the rotating fan I put in the window. I had just found a reasonable position of comfort and was drifting off to dreamland when the phone rang right by my ear. Startled, I fumbled in the dark for the phone.

"Hullo."

"Dan?"

What the hell? Why was my friend calling in the middle of the night? My mouth felt like cotton as I answered, "Yeah, it's me. What's up?"

"Dan, I hate to call you so late but you need to know that Louie Garcia and Jeff Cordova were shot and killed on north Main Street."

I jolted upright in bed. My palms were slick and I felt like I had been rabbit-punched. "My God! Did you say shot? How the hell did that happen?"

My friend's voice was shaky. "I don't know yet. From what I just heard two cops shot them after they were stopped for something."

All I could think to ask next was, "Why? Do you know why?"

The voice on the other end of the line was hard and bitter. "Since when do they need a reason to shoot one of us?" As you have probably guessed, there were no people of color on the police force or in any other public office at the time.

I was aware of an ache forming behind my eyes. "Who all was in the car?"

"I am not positive, Dan, but I heard it was Grimaldo, Louis, Jeff, someone called Hammer, and a girl. Grimaldo was driving."

I exploded into the phone. "Damn it! Damn it all! Well, hell, I am not surprised by this. With all the hassling and getting stopped for no apparent reason, just because we are Mexicans, something had to give sooner or later. Jesu Christo! This is going to get real ugly. I don't think the people will take it anymore and the shit, por favor, perdón my language, has finally hit the fan."

"I know Dan, it's going to get rough, and it's time we do something. However, there is not much we can do tonight. I just wanted you to know right away."

I thanked my friend. "Sounds like a plan. We should have more information later and can see more clearly what we have to do then."

It was ninety degrees and I was drenched in a cold sweat. I could not get back to sleep; my brain was in overdrive with bizarre pictures forming of blood and shouting and riots. They were going north on Main and the cops stopped them and somehow shot them? Just shot them?! What the hell is going on? This has got to be pure crap.

Although shaken, I knew deep down in my gut that the inevitable had occurred and there was no turning back. I looked down at my hands and realized they were clenched into fists so tightly that my brown knuckles were white. How ironic, my knuckles were "white."

My God, it looked for sure like it was going to get really wild this time. No mas! No more! Damn it, no friggin' mas! I was on my feet shouting to the moths in the dark, "Hell, I've had it! I'm done! Our people don't deserve this type of nonsense. We have been treated so badly for so long but no mas. We will not take it anymore. It's time to get in their faces! Time to change the scene! Time to rewrite the play!"

The next day the front-page headline in the local paper read, "Two Longmont Men Killed by Police." That was it. Within days after the shootings, hundreds of us gathered, some with signs on our backs that read, "Don't Shoot." We bonded together, many of us forming deep-seated, lasting relationships. We all committed to work together as a team, asserting we would no longer tolerate this racist bullshit. Our motto was, "No mas!"

As it turned out this incident would be the catalyst that would alter the course of my life forever. At the time I couldn't even guess at the personal upheaval and the consequences that this shattering event would have on me, probably just as well.

This shooting would cloud my previous ambitions and lead me to a place of prominence in my community. (I would eventually be the first person of color to be elected Councilman at Large, and after that Mayor Pro Tem.) It plunked me solidly on the path of activism, a path I walk to this day. With all the notoriety and glory I was receiving at the time, there was also the planting of a small seed of self-loathing that I would have to examine much later as to why I did some of the things I did. The results were usually very good ones for our people and for that I was grateful, but only I knew that all of my motives were not all that honorable. Some were for my own advancement. What a hell of an emotional price I was going to pay down the road. Oh, Mama, what a mess I made of me! I felt like there were two Dan's. Which of them was the real me?

I looked over at my mother, for once sleeping comfortably in the Beast. I could not resist: I reached up and smoothed a piece of hair on her forehead. She stirred, but did not waken.

Longmont: Police and emergency medical techs work to resuscitate and administer to the two shooting victims who died that fateful August night.

Photo courtesy Longmont Times Call

Friends support a family member in grief and shock after attending hearings on the fatal shootings.

Photo courtesy Longmont Times Call

Chapter 13

"Few will have the greatness to bend history itself; but each
of us can work to change a small portion of events,
and in the total of all those acts will be written
the history of this generation."

Robert F. Kennedy

How was it that I became so caught up in it all? How
was it I was the one who would be called that hot summer
night? Why me? Looking back I realized that I was a rather
highly visible Latino figure in Longmont. I ran for the school
board and lost, I put my name in the nomination ring for an
open seat on the city council but was not selected, I became
a member of the Elks, I lived on the west side of town, had
a respectable professional job, and was even the Air Traffic
Control Center's Equal Employment Officer. Yessiree, all that
gave me press and visibility. I was beginning to be somewhat
of a big fish in our small town pond.

To no one's surprise in our neck of the woods, news of the
shootings spread through the papers and news media locally
as well as outside Colorado, as other states picked up on such
a racially newsworthy event. It wasn't long before my phone
was ringing with offers of support from all over the place.
How did they get my number and so fast? The majority of
those calling would say things like, "Dan, let us help you.
This is a major civil rights event. This is good for all our
people, good to help end discrimination." Or inviting me
to make it even bigger: "Dan, we can make this a civil rights

showcase for the entire country." Wow! I thought to myself, this is major stuff here!

Then there were a few others who were not really interested in offering any positive help but contributing their two cents anyway, suggesting we let the damn city burn. And they did not mince words about: "Burn, baby, burn!" I thanked them all for their ideas and must confess to you now that I may have had a thought or two of my own of a pyromaniac nature. How friggin' sick was that? I can now acknowledge that it was what it was; I felt what I felt and, most importantly, did not act on it. Nor did I encourage any of the Latino community to go that direction.

Those were tumultuous times and I was caught up in it, the chaos that was building, and there was no doubt I was deeply involved. The rollercoaster was clicking its way to the top of the first big plunge, my mind was going in several directions at once, and I was having trouble controlling the momentum. Everybody, it seemed, wanted a piece of "the Dan." The question was whether I could satisfy both sides and still maintain the goodwill of my people. But wait, isn't the whole community supposed to be "my people?" Not everyone thought so. Perhaps it would be, "Let's watch Dan get drawn and quartered."

Within days, we, the new activists, gathered in the basement of the local Catholic Church, where we agreed to meet with the city attorney and other prominent citizens. In a room filled with palpable tension, we sat discussing our needs, the words flying like bullets across the room as we sat forward in our seats, gesturing to make our points. It was getting a little heated when the lights suddenly went out, plunging us into darkness.

Oh shit! What the hell was going on? Who did this? *Oh man, this is it,* I thought, and searched the darkness for a place to hide. The darkness also stopped all the voices for a few seconds while everyone tried to gather their bearings and, like me, fought the urge to panic. I do remember someone speaking into the silence urging us to just keep calm. We'd be okay if we just kept calm.

This was another Gandhi moment. Still, I was squirming in my seat. *Are you nuts? Keep calm?* I imagined blows or something awful coming at me. My desire to hit the floor and crawl under something was all-consuming. So much for Dan, the brave, calm local hero. And yet that voice of calm, whoever it belonged to, was like a beacon, and we homed in on it.

Within minutes the lights came back on. It turned out to be a simple power glitch that affected more than just our building. We did not know that at the time, though. Things could have gotten really nasty and that was frightening to think about later. It also made me realize that I was becoming pretty paranoid, something that, until that moment, I would have never admitted. My deep gratitude goes out to that person who kept his head when the rest of us might just as easily have lost ours.

As the meeting progressed, a city official asked us what it was we specifically wanted. Are you kidding? Well, for starters, what do you call what happened with those cops if not harassment? And the city was even going to pay for the legal expenses for the rookie. Excuse me! What the hell was that about? The room erupted with arguments slicing back and forth until it was difficult to hear anyone. Finally it ended. No one was hurt, but nothing was really resolved, either. It felt like a token meeting with no real meat to it. Yet it was a first step. We got to speak up and be heard.

But enough talk, dammit. It was time we showed that our intentions were sincere and we demanded justice. I let it be known publicly it was time to gather and march on city hall to make our statement of "No mas!" Our purpose in doing this would reveal in a very public way we would no longer put up with the harassment, the discrimination, and being treated like second-class citizens.

The movement was about to start and things were going to get hairy. Little did I know at the time that this event would become the "cause célèbre" for the rights of the Latino people in the sleepy little community of Longmont, and that this would become the most notable event of its kind in the history of our state. Just like that, we were planning to march on city hall. News traveled fast and two days later I received a call.

"Hello."

"Hello, is this Dan Benavidez?"

"Yes, it is."

The man identified himself. I recognized him as a prominent and influential member of the community. "Dan, several others who live in the city are here with me as I make this call. We are deeply concerned about the shootings and are worried that what is happening in our city could get out of control. We would really like to meet with you privately to talk about this and figure out a way we can work together to help resolve this crisis. We sincerely want to help you and the Hispanic people in our community seek the justice you all deserve and I want you to know that I believe we can do this together. We recognize you as one of the leaders of this movement, so would you agree to meet with us?"

How could I refuse?

When I arrived at the meeting I looked around at those present. Whoa! These were some of the city's most influential people. It hit me: *Oh my God! This is really important and they wanted to meet only with me?* I sure hoped my palms wouldn't sweat while I was shaking hands.

The man who called me started the meeting off with, "Dan, as I said on the phone, we're very concerned that this march could get out of hand and people might get hurt. Are you still planning to march to the city council meeting at city hall? If so, how many do you think will be marching?"

I gazed around at those present and attempted to remain calm, or at least look it. "Yes, we are still going to march. There will be hundreds of us, and we for damn sure do not want any violence to occur. Our intention is that this be a peaceful march. But what about you? What do you want?"

"Dan, I promise you that we will do all that is possible, and that includes talking to city officials, to make sure nothing bad happens. You can count on it."

I breathed a sigh of relief. "Okay, then. I will keep you informed as things move along, and I hope you will keep me in the loop so that we can make this thing go smoothly."

My host stood and shook my hand. "Thank you, Dan. Our whole community is at stake here and if we team together I believe we can deal with this horrible incident and have it turn out positively for all of us."

"Follow me! Follow me!" Over a hundred of us had gathered with lighted candles at the church about two blocks from city hall. I shouted once again, "Follow me! Peacefully! Follow me! It's *our* time! It's time we let them know we want justice!" I started singing, "We Shall Overcome." As others joined in, we held our candles and began our march.

We had moved barely a block when I thought I noticed something out of the ordinary. Whoa! Was my imagination running wild? No, I didn't think so. What the hell were those cops doing on top of the buildings? And damn if it didn't look like they had guns. Were those rifles? Yes, I was sure—they had rifles.

Oh God! I hoped they really were cops. What if they shot at us? This could be ugly beyond words. Man, someone could get hurt after all, and I'm responsible for these people. They chose to follow me. I had the chills and started shaking all over. I put a determined smile on my face and hoped no one would see how scared I was. My mind began a crazy mental dance. Is this really the right thing to do? I am out in front of the pack. Will they shoot me first?

I had to do some really quick self-assurance. *Okay, okay, calm down. I am here and I'm not going to quit. Can't do that, not now, so no matter what happens I am in this. Onward. Onward.* I sang louder. "We shall overcome!" Oh mi Dios, I hope we will be okay!

It turned out that the march was a huge success. We flooded the city council chamber and made our demands peacefully to the mayor and city council. One thing you can say for sure, we got their attention.

"Dad, the postman brought a box for you!" Celia shouted up the stairs.

"Okay, CC, I'll be right down." I sauntered down and picked up the box. Inside was a beautifully wrapped package. *How nice,* I thought. *Someone sent me a gift, probably thanking me for leading the march.* I was feeling pretty special. CC was excited too.

"Go on and open it, Dad." I carefully peeled back the lovely wrapping paper so that we could save it and peered inside the smaller box. Our smiles turned to horror and shock as we looked at a box full of human feces. The "love note" said, "Here is a shitty gift for a shitty person. Beware!"

CC put a hand over her mouth. "Oh my, Daddy! How awful!" My daughter's expression turned fearful. That she had to witness this ugly and cowardly display of rage was despicable. That it frightened her made it all the worse. I was seething but could not let her see. "Dad, will you be okay? Who would do this?" There were tears in her eyes.

I put my arms around my daughter to reassure her. "I don't know, CC, and yes, I am okay. Please don't worry. I will try to find out what's going on, but honey, I want you to do your best to not let this get to you, all right?" She nodded but I could tell she wasn't buying it.

Several days later I heard from one of the men I originally met with from the city and it was encouraging to hear his voice. "Dan, it's me. I just wanted you to know that I heard from a reliable source that the John Birch Society is looking closely at what is going on here. Believe me, Dan, the people who sent you that horrible 'gift' are serious, so please be careful and remember we are doing all we can to keep the peace in our community. I am pleading with you to remember your promise to not let this get out of control. Like it or not, you are at the top of the heap, so let's do our best to keep it in Longmont. Oh, and you may have noticed there is a police car parked at the end of your block just as reassurance for you."

I swallowed past the lump in my throat. It had really started now. I thanked my friend and reassured him of my intent to keep it local, and promised again to keep him in the loop for any more news or unwelcome packages.

The calls kept coming, now from outside Longmont from bigger and better known activists.

"Dan, this is Jose." (Name changed to protect the "active.") "Do you know who I am?" Holy crap, this guy was big. And he heard about ME? They were coming out of the woodwork.

"Yes, Jose, I know who you are! And I am honored you would be calling me."

"Thank you, Dan. Just about everybody knows what is going on in Longmont. This is a major happening. We would like to help you. Can you meet with us? I was thinking we could meet in Frederick on Thursday night at eight."

I could hardly breathe. "Yes, I would like very much to meet with you and your people."

Jose then gave me directions. "Okay, just drive down I-25 to County Road 22 and on down until it turns into Sable Avenue to Frontier Street which is on the corner of Central Park. We will meet you there. When you get there pull up behind our car and blink your lights twice." What? This sounded like such cloak-and-dagger shit.

But I replied, "Great, that will work. I'll see you there."

He must have heard the hesitation in my voice because he added, "Dan, you may or may not know that someone placed what I heard was some type of bomb under a car in the underground parking lot at the Civic Center. We can't be too careful. This is getting ugly and could escalate."

I did not need to be told that. "Yes, Jose, I heard about it, and I know this is bad shit, but I don't think this is getting

any more out of control than it presently is. From what I heard
this was some unknown individual who did this, not one of
us. But it is for sure a hell of a mess and I have to tell you I
am getting a little spooked by the thought that someone may
try to 'off' me."

The night of the secret meeting was black, no stars in the
sky. Damn, why did I agree to this clandestine rendezvous?
Who else knows about it? Are there eyes and ears everywhere?
God help me! I drove up to the corner of Sable and Frontier,
saw a car parked there, pulled up behind it, and blinked my
lights twice and held my breath. Someone I could not see
clearly got out of the car and walked back to me. I rolled down
my window and looked at the shadowy figure standing there.

"Dan, is that you?" Jose leaned down and I exhaled.

"Yes, it's me."

"Glad you could make it. Come join us in my car."

I followed him to his car and got in the front passenger
side next to Jose. There were two others in the back seat and
they introduced themselves. Jose didn't waste any time with
small talk.

"Dan, you have a real crisis going on in Longmont, so I
will get right to the point. We saw you in the papers and on
television leading the march. It's a great thing you are doing
here. Were you threatened during the march?" One of the
guys in the back piped in, "I bet you were, huh? We know
about the bomb under the car, too." Jose continued, "Dan
we want to be part of this. This is definitely a major civil
rights event that we can take nationwide. I assure you we can
make it happen if you want us to. We are ready to come to
Longmont and get this going, so let's do it!"

I was feeling hopeful and also a bit overwhelmed by what
he was suggesting. "Look, Jose, I am sure you can, and I am
flattered. But I have to tell you that at one point in the march
I thought we were being threatened when I saw guys on the
rooftops with guns. Turned out they were cops there to protect
us in case something happened. I thank you for your offer, but

what I suggest is I go back to Longmont and talk it over with my people and get back to you as quickly as possible."

Jose agreed and I promised to contact him soon. I turned and thanked the other guys who assured me once again they were there to help and available to me if needed.

True to my word, I called my friend in Longmont to inform him of the latest development. He asked me if I was still hanging in there and doing okay.

"Yeah, I'm doing okay, but a little stressed out. I called to let you know I met with Jose. I believe you know about him, don't you?"

My friend did not sound exactly pleased. "Damn right I know who he is."

I went on. "He told me he wants to come help us in Longmont and make this a big nationwide civil rights event. He said he could assemble a whole bunch of people to gather in Longmont and do a major demonstration."

"Dan, like I mentioned before, I've been concerned that others would try to get involved and make a mess of it. Their motives may be pure, but more than likely they want to get involved with this only for personal notoriety. I thought we discussed and agreed to work together and keep it in Longmont where we can control things. That way we can assure that this would work out for the betterment of our community and not make it more of a major event than it already is." He paused then continued, "I know this might seem like a Catch-22 where you might feel damned if you do and damned if you don't, but you've already become a highly visible person. At this point you are viewed as a peacemaker, so please, Dan, I am asking you again, *please* do not join with them. Can we still keep this a local issue?"

I called Jose to thank him for his offering of support but explained that for now we were going to handle the situation by ourselves. I said I would call him if I needed help.

He wasn't thrilled with my decision. "Okay, Dan, but you're messing up. Believe me, you're messing up big time."

I called my contact. "Hi, this is Dan. I want you to know that I turned down the offer from Jose's group. Looks like it is going to be just us. Thanks for hanging in there with me." He sounded relieved. "Dan, to the contrary, thank you."

When all was said and done, we kept the peace and together changed the course of our city. That hot August night will always remain vividly in my mind, however, for many reasons, not the least of which it changed my life's course.

Years later I realized that, to some degree, I let my ambitions cloud my motives. I remember sitting in my car on 4th Street across from St. John's Baptist Church talking to a reporter all about it and my role as the lead in the city's first major demonstration for minority rights. I reiterated that we were not there to say please; we made it clear that change *was* going to happen. It could be peaceful, or not. I let it all hang out and even shared some of my own motives and regrets that became clearer as the years went on. Some I was proud of, some not so much. It was also the solid beginning of my own rise to some prominence within the community.

I was soon identified as the one who organized, influenced, led, and helped keep a peaceful lid on what could have been a racially violent scene. My political star was rising and I liked it. Thinking on it now, I am embarrassed when I recall how excited I was to be part of the "in crowd" of those with influence. That ingrained baggage I carried containing my Latino inferiority complex ran a lot of my external actions in those days. I would wake at night thinking I was almost "white" while immediately chanting, "Viva La Raza." What a dichotomy. I am human, a brown one, and many good things came of my actions, just not all for the best of reasons in my view. Yeah, yeah, this is getting repetitive. It was like viewing the situation in a rear-view-mirror. Somehow, this small segment of the total picture when seen as a back-to-front reflected image is always crystal clear, right? Just nod your head, okay?

Chapter 14

"Your problem is you're too busy
holding onto your own unworthiness."

Ram Dass

Six months gone and a lifetime of stories and memories
shared. Many stories I shared with Mom and many more I
kept to myself. It seemed hardly possible that it had been more
than six months since Mom's entry into the hospice program
and we were approaching the finale. The Blue Beast was gone
and in its place was a hospital bed. Blue was gone and that
love/hate relationship with that damned chair lingered and I
sort of missed that whirring sound it made when I fought to
locate that tiniest of adjustments that would alleviate her pain.
Now we were in the final days—the deathwatch. We crept
around like phantoms, watching, listening, and being there in
those rare moments she was awake and lucid.

I lay down on the couch across from the bed in the living
room. It served as the bed for us caretakers. I could not get
comfortable; it was lumpy and the pillow too spongy. I knew
every damned spot on that couch and how to squirm around
the worst lumps to find my "spot" where I could rest. Tonight
that comfy spot eluded me. My eyes felt like they had been
sprayed with mace. I was beyond tired. When I am that tired
my mind takes the upper hand and races as fast as it can to places
I normally would not let it go. Tonight it was having a field day.
I went over how far I had come and I was sort of famous, or
infamous depending on your perspective, since the shootings.

Mom saved all the newspaper clippings and it was one of the subjects she loved to talk about. I wasn't feeling as good about myself as I was when all the notoriety first hit me. Twice I tried and failed to get elected to the city's school board. After two failed attempts, I finally got elected to city council. Eventually I would be elected Mayor Pro Tem of Longmont. There was considerable press and even TV interviews. I was riding high for a Latino in a predominantly white community. I feasted on the fame. I thought, "Boy, I bet I will get into the 'right' circles now. I'll show them."

I was trying like hell to wash the brown (my friend Lyndy described my hue as mocha espresso) off my skin and be more white, more powerful, one of the "movers and shakers" of my community. In some ways I was—not more white, but a bit of a mover and a shaker. I thought it was for *all* the wrong reasons, but I see now they weren't all wrong. Some were right, and many good things came out of it for my Latino "family" and the rest of the community as well. We were slowly beginning the integration process from them-vs.-us to a more holistic "ours."

I moved my butt to a different lump on the couch and listened to Mom's ragged breaths. These six months allowed me to finally process that it's not about more "stuff," and it was not even about me. I almost lost my family while feeding my ego. I was not really all there for my daughters when their mother was brutally murdered. I held it together, but Mama came to the rescue and was really present for them and for me, just like always.

Way back in January, when we were told that Mom's cancer was terminal, I had convinced myself that I would be able to handle her death. I was the "man" and could handle anything. I had trained myself to believe I did not really need anyone. I would be the one who was needed, by my family and my community. It was a pretty good defense mechanism that made me seem attractively aloof. I thought of myself as the strong sibling, the one to call when there was a crisis. Man, did I mislead myself.

Mama was pretty open right from the beginning about her cancer. It shocked me to hear her say she accepted it and was ready to go home to God whenever He thought it was her time. I could barely talk about it even though she tried to engage me in conversation about it on several occasions. It may be she was trying to get me to face reality, or maybe she just needed to talk about it. I didn't want to listen in either case.

I told her over and over how much I loved her, and spilled my guts on many a late night asking for forgiveness for my own "sins" and actions. She was my confessor and not by her choice, but she accepted it gracefully, allowing me to come full circle in my own forgiveness. Mama knew she was going to die and she was ready for it nonetheless. I was never really ready. Yet we took a journey together, each of us to a new life, hers to a heavenly realm and me learning to live better on Earth. Caring for my dying mother made a human being of me, probably for the first time, and I was fully conscious of it. It was a most uncomfortable process, and my siblings and friends saw me and were confused many times, I am sure, by my body language and mixed signals. I am sure they were wondering if I was losing it. Perhaps I was, losing a part of me that needed to go.

In the first week of June it became clear that Mama had only a couple of weeks or less to live. The following Tuesday was my shift and I had just finished doing all the routine checks. Mom's breathing was noticeably labored and her moments of consciousness were more infrequent. All her remaining energy was spent taking the next breath.

I gave up fighting the lumps in the couch and went out back, where I spent many a night fantasizing or going over events of my life. It was my sanctuary, just me and the stars and the occasional meteor or passing satellite. I got the old plastic chair and tilted my head back, preparing to relax for a bit. But I could not get comfortable. And there were no satellites, and I could always count on one of those. Something was amiss. Even the usual neighborhood hoopla that seemed to never stop was absent, replaced by a heavy stillness. No, there was a sense

of foreboding I could not place my finger on, and I got up and
went back in the house to check on Mom.

Even though I knew where every stick of furniture was in
the house and had never had any problems navigating through
the patio doors, I managed to stub my toe on a table leg. Damn
that hurt! I swore under my breath and my eyes watered from
the pain. I immediately got angry at the table that had been
there forever and at all the ghosts that crowded into the room
with me.

What the hell am I doing there? I wondered. It was all so
depressing and miserable. What was the point? I fumbled my
way to Mama's bed. She would inhale with a rattling sound
that tore me up to hear, slowly let it out, and then I would wait
and wait, an eternity, until she would begin that slow painful
cycle yet again. In the dimness her face was ashen and her
lips a blue that made them appear almost black in the weird
lighting. My insides turned to jelly as I feared that this was
the moment. Suddenly she opened her eyes and it seemed she
recognized me until she asked, "Is that you, Lolly?"

I leaned in and grabbed her hand. "No, Mom, it's me,
Danny." She closed her eyes again.

I was tired. We all were. I went back to the couch and lay
down, mindless of the lumps. What seemed like only moments
later I was awakened by a horrible sound. I bolted off the
couch to Mom's bed where she was gurgling and struggling to
breathe. Her eyes were open wide and glassy. "Damn, Mom,
don't die on me. Don't do this now, not with me here alone!"
I called out to God to let her live through my shift. Another
embarrassing moment of truth for macho Dan. I was terrified
to be alone with my mother when she died.

My thoughts were interrupted as I remembered I was
supposed to give her a sublingual morphine tablet every two
hours to keep her comfortable. I grabbed one and tried to
rouse her.

"Mom, wake up, open your mouth, please Mom, I need to
give you your painkiller."

She struggled so very hard to open her mouth, but she could not do it. I was told to give her one no matter what or the pain would get unbearable. I put the fingers of my left hand under her upper teeth and the fingers of my right hand on her lower teeth and forced her mouth open. Working the tablet onto the right index finger I slipped it under her tongue, all the while wondering, *Why am I still doing this?* If she could not even open her mouth and does not know me, maybe she is past the pain. What good was it going to do her now?

But I held her jaw and crooned, "I won't hurt you, Mama. It will be okay. You just need your pill. Mama, please don't die, not right now. Please, just wait for Lee. She will be here real soon." My voice broke and I sobbed, "I don't think I can handle it alone, Mom. Please!"

Another rattle came from deep in her chest and she tried to turn her head to me to speak. I put my ear close to her mouth but she couldn't get any words out. She just stared blankly at me. What was she thinking? Were there thoughts? Were her thoughts already past this world? Was she wondering who this babbling idiot was by the bed worried about things that no longer had any real significance? I may never know, but maybe one day when I leave this world, I will meet up with her for some heavenly chili and beans and ask her.

Then she suddenly became lucid and looked right at me. "What time is it, hijo? Is it daylight yet?" Just like that she whispered those words in my ear. I was shocked. She struggled to speak again: "When will Ted be here?" Then she peacefully shut her eyes.

It turned out those were her last words. I did not hear any breath. I put my face close to her mouth to see if I could feel a breath. I whispered, "Mom, are you dead?" Fear was taking hold of me. Not now. Not with me, no. Then I felt her faint breath on my cheek and I sighed in relief.

I went back to the couch and in my exhaustion and confusion thought the most absurd thought. Maybe I should get her up to go to the potty. Maybe if I sat her up she could breathe better. *Good God, Dan, you are really losing it now. This is it, it is happening and all you need to do is be here and be strong. Fake it if you have to.*

I looked over on the stand next to the bed and noticed the little hand bell Jenny gave her some time back to use when she needed something. Mom said it reminded her of her childhood days and the school bells that the teacher used to call them in. Mom never went past the fourth grade. She would try to shake that bell as gently as possible, as if in apology for being an inconvenience, for having to go to the bathroom or needing some adjustment when the pain got too bad. I resented that damn bell. I could not sleep well because I was waiting for it to ring in the middle of the night. How impatient I was. Yeah, I would give anything to see her have the strength to sit up and ring the shit out of that bell now. But the bell sat silent. It had nothing more to say.

Around three in the morning I was awakened yet again by a different sound from the bed. It was a long surrealistic rattling sigh, "Aagggaaaaaaaaaaa." Once again I jumped up in a panic and put my ear next to her mouth, praying to God and all the saints and angels to let her last a little longer, while at the same time begging forgiveness of those same saints and angels for my weakness and fear of not being able to let her go. Yes, there was one more breath.

I crawled back to the couch and fell immediately asleep. When I woke it was eight a.m. *Oh God, is she still alive?* I went over to the bed, and, yes, she was still breathing, though barely. Thank you, God.

My sister arrived close to nine and I was never so glad to see anyone in my life. I could have hugged her. She asked how the night went as we sat over a cup of coffee.

"It was bad, very bad, sis. I thought for sure Mom died a couple of times." My sister sipped her coffee and just looked at me. I could hardly meet her gaze. "Damn it, I know you must think I'm a real horse's ass, the way I've been strutting around here and acting like I can handle anything, but I have to admit I cannot take much more of this. I can't!" I nearly broke down and sobbed.

My sister put down her cup. "Oh, Danny, don't feel bad. You are human like the rest of us and we are all stretched pretty thin. This can't last much longer, maybe only hours. Who knows?" I looked at my sister realizing in that moment how much she was going through as well. And yet she held it and us together.

We got up and walked over to Mom's bed. She was completely unconscious now. I leaned in and gave her a kiss, gathered up my stuff and said goodbye. Although she needed no such instructions, I told Lee to call when-or-if, and headed to my office.

I hadn't been at my desk long when Lori shouted, "Dan, telephone! It sounds like your sister and she is upset." I knew what was coming.

"Yeah, sis. Mom died, right?"

Lee was crying hard. "Yes, Danny, she died a few minutes ago."

Our mother died Wednesday, June 11, 1996, at 10:02 AM. It was just the thing she would do: Spare me that moment I so feared and wanted to avoid. So I had to live with that and yes, my friends, I felt cheated and forever guilty about it. But that was that. The phone rang on my desk and I remember looking at it wondering why it just kept ringing. Finally, I picked it up and snapped into the receiver, "My mom just died. Leave me alone!"

To this day I don't know who it was and no one came forward. If it was a friend, then I trust they understood. If it was a stranger, then I am sure he was shocked and I could have cared less. I made it out to the parking lot on a beautiful warm day and just broke down with my head in my hands. I was oblivious to anyone who might be walking by or in the lot and no one approached me. I could have been invisible.

I got myself somewhat under control in the two miles to Bowen Street, where I met Jody from hospice and my sisters at the house. I walked in and realized it had been just a little over an hour since I left her.

My sister met me. "She's gone, Dan." I looked down at Mama's face.

"Goodbye, Mamacita, my precious, my teacher, and my strength. You alone helped me with my demons and now I am alone, your macho son. I love you." Then I began my litany, the words just tumbling out of me. "O Lord, hear my voice. Let your ears be attentive to my voice in supplication. If you, Lord, mark iniquities, Lord, who can stand? But with you is forgiveness that you revered. I trust the Lord. My soul trusts in His word. My soul awaits for the Lord more than sentinels wait for the dawn." I realized I was muttering some of the passages from the Psalm of the Dead, the De Profundis. I did not even know I remembered it, and I spoke the words for my mother and for myself. Part of me had died as well. If I allowed it, I could wash myself clean of my own demons and the self-loathing.

My mother was free, and it was time to make some decisions about myself or the last six months would be for naught. I made a promise to my mother: My journey was still ahead of me; what would I make of it? It was all so fresh—the smells of the sick room, the air on the patio, the steely gaze of my mother's dark eyes when she knew what was truly in my heart. I had only to shut my eyes and it all came back. Now there was this void. What would I fill it with?

Even though I was never that far from my mother for most of my life, it had only been in the last five or so years that I really spent quality time with her and got to know who she was, what she wanted, her dreams. We learned much about each other, I think. She always had more confidence in me than I did and never judged me for my decisions. I do know she was shocked and not a little disappointed when I admitted I was ashamed of my Mexican heritage. She forgave me, though, a lot quicker than I forgave myself.

Mom showed me how to love. She modeled how one could rise above almost any situation life throws at you and make something good out of it. She had a hard life and many unfulfilled dreams as a young girl, yet she never lost her pride, even when my father lost his. She showed me that "stuff" just isn't it. And I know, because I had lots of stuff at one time and it did not make me happy, just overstuffed. My Canadian friend, Ken, pointed out to me that you don't need more stuff to change the world, just passion, persistence, and dedication to a cause that is close to your heart. Remember Ghandi?

Every now and then I allow myself to feel disappointment that Mom did not live long enough to see the human being I am today, more loving and hopefully more conscious of doing things for the right reasons. But then again, maybe she does.

Epilogue

Well I've run through rainbows and castles of candy,
I cried a river of tears from the pain,
I try to dance with what life has to hand me,
My partner's been pleasure, my partner's been pain.

There are days when I swear I could fly like an eagle,
And dark desperate hours that nobody sees.
My arms stretched triumphant on top of the mountain,
My head in my hands down on my knees.

You got to take it as it comes.
Sometimes it don't come easy.

Sometimes it's a bitch,
Sometimes it's a breeze.

Stevie Nicks

Dear Mom,

I think you would be proud of me now, mi angel dulce.
Wait, I can almost see you rolling your eyes at me. Let me
start over. I am now able to see the good parts of me and be
proud of them. Back then I just could not understand it all
and I did not have the eyes to really see who I was and that the
journey I was on was perfect for me.

I still have my moments of doubt and there are certainly
challenges and choices in front of me that make me pause.
At least I am more aware of my choices and can accept

responsibility for them. And I am thinking I make more of them for the right reasons.

You always told me I was a good boy. Why couldn't I hear you? I see lots of reasons and it certainly was no fault of yours. You brought me up in a caring Mexican family immersed in the culture of our heritage. Within my little family I was okay. Outside of it the things I saw and heard created self-doubt and insecurities. As a young boy I determined that, in order to be anyone substantial in this world, I would have to somehow be more white. The key to wealth, in my view, lay in the white majority.

My attention became riveted on the fact that we never had much stuff like the Anglos, could not choose where we wanted to live, belong to private clubs, or hold public office. I was obsessed with the desire to be more Anglo because that was where power, security, and privilege lay. Dad unwittingly reinforced that notion when he told Bobby and me to say we were Spanish, not Mexican. And, Mama, I don't blame Dad for that. He had his own demons to deal with.

Eventually, I got what I thought I wanted: fame, entry into once-forbidden clubs, public office, and leadership. I never said no if I thought it would advance me up the ladder of success into the realm of what I perceived was Anglo power. I nearly killed myself as an overachiever—for all the wrong reasons.

My time with you during your last months allowed me to untangle myself and clean out that cesspool that kept me from just being me. What was left was this empty space, and you showed me how to fill it with more "stuff," good stuff. Danny became brown again—or mocha espresso—and it was good, really good. I wasn't alone in a sea of white faces. I was me in the middle of a community and I mattered, not because they thought so, but because I thought so.

It is no longer important if I am invited to their big parties. It is okay either way. If they are friends, fine; that matters more. If I can make a difference by sitting on a board or participating in a cause and it gladdens my heart to do it, then I am there 100%. I realize that some want me now *because* of my Mexican heritage and the things I have done. Amazing, huh? The difference is, I belong, join, or participate because I believe it is the right thing to do, for the right cause, and right for me.

It all comes down to the simple fact that you are what you are, and you modeled that beautifully, Mamacita. You never groveled, you made the best with what you had, and held your head high. You made sacrifices for all the right reasons, for the love of your family, and you never made excuses. You can never wash off the color of your skin or whatever it is you think makes you feel inferior. You can do a lot of housekeeping on the inside where it matters most. You kept a clean house, Mom, and I am really attempting to do the same. It is a daily chore.

I will no longer strive to be a "good Mexican." I am just a Mexican, a good man who cares about his community. Mama, I love you, and will be forever grateful for the lessons and the love you provided. Know that I carry you in my heart and your chili recipe in my kitchen. It is my connection with you when I spoon chili and beans with a soft tortilla. And if you are watching, Mama, tell me, just one more time: How many fingers am I holding up?

Tu hijo,

Danny

CPSIA information can be obtained
at www.ICGtesting.com
Printed in the USA
FSOW02n2327300517
34646FS